The Masses Arise

The Great French Revolution
1789-1815

by Peter Taaffe

Fortress

This book has been rushed out and published against all the odds to coincide with the 200th anniversary of the French revolution. This was only made possible by the help and unstinting work of the following who I would like to thank; Dianne Mitchell for her unflagging and excellent work in typing. Kevin Parslow, for research and reading, and Tony Aitman for his Herculean efforts at research, suggestions and labours in ensuring that this book saw the light of day.

Peter Taaffe
2 June 1989

The Masses Arise
The Great French Revolution 1789-1815
by Peter Taaffe

First edition June 1989
Published by Fortress Books,
PO Box 141, London E2 ORL (01-985-7394)
Printed by Biddles of Guildford and Kings Lynn

ISBN 1 870958 07

Cover design by Richard Evans

Fortress Books is a socialist publishing house. We encourage readers of our works to actively participate in the struggle for socialism. If you would like to receive more information about the ideas and events in this book, or have any comments and suggestions, you are welcome to contact the author via Fortress Books, PO Box 141, London E2 ORL

Contents

Paris in 1790

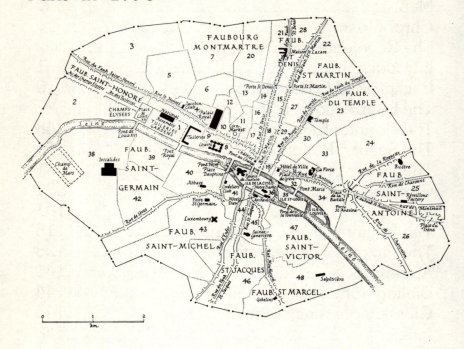

The Sections

1 Tuileries	13 Fontaine Montmorency	25 Montreuil	37 Henri IV
2 Champs Élysées	14 Bonne Nouvelle	26 Quinze-Vingts	38 Invalides
3 Roule	15 Ponceau	27 Gravilliers	39 Fontaine de Grenelle
4 Palais Royal	16 Mauconseil	28 Faub. Saint-Denis	40 Quatre Nations
5 Place Vendôme	17 Marché des Innocents	29 Beaubourg	41 Théâtre Français
6 Bibliothèque	18 Lombards	30 Enfants Rouges	42 Croix Rouge
7 Grange Batelière	19 Arcis	31 Roi de Sicile	43 Luxembourg
8 Louvre	20 Faub Montmartre	32 Hôtel de Ville	44 Thermes de Julien
9 Oratoire	21 Poissonnière	33 Place Royale	45 Sainte-Geneviève
10 Halle au Blé	22 Bondy	34 Arsenal	46 Observatoire
11 Postes	23 Temple	35 Ile Saint-Louis	47 Jardin des Plantes
12 Place Louis XIV	24 Popincourt	36 Notre-Dame	48 Gobelins

Chronology of key events 1788-1799

1788

8 August	Announcement of recall of Estates General
25 September	Paris *parlement* recommends Estates General should be constituted as in 1614
6 November	Assembly of Notables meets

1789

28-29 April	Revellion riots
5 May	Estates General meet at Versailles
17 June	Third Estate adopts title of National Assembly
19 June	Majority of clergy vote to join Third Estate
20 June	Tennis Court Oath
26 June	Troops begin to concentrate around Paris
27 June	King orders clergy and nobility to join the Third Estate
12-17 July	Riots in Paris
14 July	Fall of the Bastille
15 July	King received at Hôtel de Ville. Forced to adopt tricolour cockade
July-August	The Great Fear
4 August	Renunciation of feudal rights in National Assembly
26 August	Declaration of Rights of Man and of the Citizen
5 October	March of women to Versailles
6 October	Royal Family brought to Paris followed by National Assembly
29 October	'Active' and 'Passive' citizens distinguished by decree
2 November	Church property nationalised
7 November	decree excluding deputies from Ministry

1790

13 February	Religious orders, except those engaged in teaching or charitable work, suppressed
19 June	Titles of hereditary nobility abolished

1791

20 June	Flight to Varennes
25 June	King suspended from his functions on being brought back to Paris
17 July	The 'Massacre of the Champ de Mars'
14 September	King accepts Constitution and is restored to functions

1 October	Legislative Assembly meets
9 November	Decree ordering return to France of *émigrés* suspected of conspiracy against nation
12 November	King vetos decree against the *émigrés*

1792

9 February	Property of *émigrés* decreed forfeit to nation
10 March	Assembly brings about resignation of Ministry; replaced by administration sympathetic to Girondins
20 April	War declared
19 June	King vetos proposed military camp near Paris
20 June	Invasion of Tuileries
11 July	Decree of '*La patrie en danger*'
25-30 July	Arrival of *fédéres* from Brest and Marseilles
3 August	All but one of the Paris *sections* petition for deposition of King
9 August	Insurrectionary commune formed in Paris
10 August	Storming of the Tuileries
11 August	King suspended from functions
19 August	Lafayette defects to Austrians
23 August	Longwy falls to Prussians
25 August	Redemption charges for seigneurial dues abolished
2-6 September	Prison massacres
20 September	Convention constituted
21 September	Convention abolishes monarchy
22 September	Convention decrees that all acts from now on are to be dated from Year 1 of the Republic
6 November	French army advances into Belgium

1793

14-7 January	Convention debates fate of King
21 January	The King is executed
1 February	War declared against England and Holland
7 March	War declared against Spain
10 March	Revolutionary Tribunal established
11 March	Revolt in La Vendée begins
21 March	*Comités de surveillance* established in every commune
26 March	Committee of Public Safety formed
13 April	Marat arraigned before Revolutionary Tribunal
4 May	First *maximum*
May-October	Federalist revolts in provinces against the

	Convention
28 May	Insurrectionary Committee formed
29 May-2 June	Overthrow of the Girondins
5 June	Couthon, Saint-Just and Herault de Sechelles join Committee of Public Safety
24 June	Constitution of 1793
13 July	Murder of Marat
17 July	Final abolition of all feudal rights without compensation
27 July	Robespierre joins Committee of Public Safety
28 July	Fall of Valenciennes
23 August	Decree of *levée en masse*
5 September	Attempted coup by Hebertists
29 September	Law of General *maximum*
7 October	Adoption of Revolutionary Calendar: Year II deemed to have begun on 22 September
9 October	Lyons retaken
16 October	Marie Antoinette executed
31 October	Girondin leaders executed
6 November	Duc d'Orléans executed
8 November	Madame Roland executed
11 November	Bailly executed
29 November	Barnave executed
19 December	English evacuate Toulon
23 December	*Vendéens* defeated at Savenay

1794

24 March	Execution of Hébertists
2 April	Danton's trial begins
5 April	Execution of Dantonists
8 June	Festival of the Supreme Being
26 July	Robespierre calls for purge in his last speech in the Convention
27 July	*Journée* of 9 *Thermidor* Arrest of Robespierrists Abolition of Paris Commune by Convention
28-9 July	Execution of Robespierre and his followers
30-31 July	Reorganisation of Committee of Public Safety
31 July	*Maximum des salaires* withdrawn
10 August	Reorganisation of Revolutionary Tribunal
12 November	Jacobin Club closed
24 December	*Maximum* abolished

1795

21 February	Decree separating Church and State
23 May	Parisian *sections* disarmed
May-June	The White Terror
22 July	Peace with Spain signed
22 August	Convention approves Constitution of the Year III
4-6 October	*Journées* of *Vendémiaire*
26 October	Convention is dissolved
	Directory is inaugurated

1796

2 March	Bonaparte becomes General of the Army of Italy
10 May	Bonaparte defeats Austrians at Lodi

1797

27 May	Babeuf executed

1799

9 October	Bonaparte lands at Frejus
9 November	*Coup d'état* of 18 *Brumaire*

The Revolutionary Calendar

The revolutionary calendar was used from 22 Sept 1793 (1 Vendemaire of Year II of the revolution) until the end of 1805.

Vendemiare	Sept 22-Oct 21
Brumaire	Oct 22-Nov 20
Frimaire	Nov 21-Dec 20
Nivose	Dec 21-Jan 19
Pluviose	Jan 20-Feb 18
Ventose	Feb 19-Mar 20
Germinal	Mar 21-Apr 19
Floreal	Apr 20-May 19
Prairial	May 20-Jun 18
Messidor	Jun 19-Jul 18
Thermidor	Jul 19-Aug 17
Fructidor	Aug 18-Sep 16

At the end of the revolutionary calendar were 5 or 6 days known as Sans-culottides, from Sep 17-21

Introduction

THE GREAT FRENCH revolution was to the Europe of the late eighteenth century and the first part of the nineteenth century what the Russian revolution is to the twentieth century. It was the third major capitalist (bourgeois) revolution, preceded by the English revolution of the seventeenth century and the American revolution of 1776. But it had a much greater impact than its predecessors and was, up to then, the single greatest event in human history.

The immortal poet Shelley later wrote that it was 'the master theme of the epoch'. It had a convulsive effect in Europe. It detonated movements of the black slaves in France's colonial empire, and it even affected events in the young American republic. The tyrants of Europe, all the kings, princes and tsars feared for their thrones. Feudal and semi-feudal Europe ganged up with the British capitalists in a coalition to snuff out the contagious effects of the revolution.

The international effects

From its outset, the French revolution evoked the greatest interest and support throughout Europe. The majority of artists and intellectuals rallied to the revolution. Those like Edmund Burke, chief propagandist of the counter-revolution, who published his 'Reflections on the Revolution in France' in November 1790, were initially drowned out in the chorus of support which seemed to sweep through Europe in the wake of the revolution. The great German philosopher Hegel hailed the revolution as that 'superb sunrise over Europe'. He was joined by the philosophers Kant and Fichte, as well as the giant composer Beethoven.

The revolution seemed to sweep the whole of intellectual and

1

artistic Germany before it. Only Bavaria, under the heel of the Jesuits, seemed to resist the attractions of the revolution. And it was not just intellectuals, but the masses of Germany who were touched by the revolution. Thus the bourgeoisie of Hamburg celebrated the fall of the Bastille in 1790. Strikes also broke out in the same city in 1791. In the Rhineland the masses, touched by the revolution and stirred up by famine, challenged the authority of the governing oligarchies. There were uprisings in many towns and the peasants, emulating the French provinces along the Rhine, refused to pay feudal fees. This movement spread into the very depths of Germany, in some areas resembling France's earlier peasant uprisings, the *jacqueries*.

Belgium, which, before the French revolution, had witnessed uprisings of workers and peasants, rose after an initial delay. This started in Liege, under the leadership of Vonck, who took Ghent and Mons, and this in turn led to an uprising in Brussels. In December 1789, the Vonckists drove the Austrians from their Belgian provinces. The contagion spread to German Switzerland, to Geneva and to Savoy where the peasants were refusing to pay redemption fees when manorial rights were suppressed.

Feudal reaction on a European scale took to the road of repression. The British bourgeoisie on the other hand initially took an ambivalent position. With that patrician arrogance for which they were famous, they offered to help the 'lesser breed without the law', in this case the French, in their 'constitutional experiments'. Some of the bourgeois like Fox, while expressing sympathy for the revolution, also drew up schemas with the French constitutional monarchist Mirabeau, for the transplanting of Britain's constitutional system onto French soil. After all, the 'constitutional monarchy' was the quintessence of progress and enlightenment for the British bourgeois. Others, like the calculating Pitt, however saw France's difficulties—'revolutionary convulsions'—as England's opportunity to steal markets, colonial possessions etc.

The earlier relatively neutral and benevolent approach of the British bourgeoisie was, however, to give way to implacable opposition as the revolution advanced. Its impact on the British masses—as well as in its own 'backyard' in Ireland—terrified the British bourgeoisie. Its attitude was summed up in the policies of William Pitt, who, in combatting the French revolution, exercised a thinly veiled personal dictatorship.

Through Pitt, the British bourgeoisie was to learn invaluable lessons in combatting the threat of revolution. It was in the struggle

2

against the revolution that Pitt evolved those policies of combining repression with concessions which were to serve the British bourgeoisie so well in the future.

To begin with, as in other countries, British intellectuals and artists were in ecstasy over the French revolution. Wordsworth penned his famous poem *Prelude*, Coleridge and the immortal Robert Burns joined in. Others were to turn their back on the revolution later, but Burns and the Scottish democrats remained firm. In 1792, Robert Burns purchased cannons to send to the French and on one occasion rose from a theatre seat to call for *Ca ira*. This was a revolutionary song, the words of which went: *Ca ira, ca ira, ca ira! Les aristocrates à la lanterne!*—'Here we go, here we go, here we go! Hang the aristocrats from the lamppost!'. The English poets such as Wordsworth continued to express support for the revolution even after the execution of the king. His sentiments were expressed in *The Borderers*, as were Southey's in the play *Wat Tyler*. However, they were ostracised from 'respectable society', became discouraged, and eventually turned their backs on the revolution. By 1794 Coleridge and Southey 'wept over their broken dreams', while the former actually celebrated the fall of Robespierre. For this he earned the scorn of all British democrats. Shelley twenty years later excoriated him for his betrayal.

However, the British workers proved to be far more enduring than the intellectuals. At the outbreak of the revolution, clubs had mushroomed in Britain. By 1792, 30 popular societies existed in Norwich, and in Sheffield 5000 enrolled in these societies. Thomas Paine, veteran of the American revolution and future member of the French Convention, in which he supported the Gironde, wrote his famous reply to Edmund Burke, 'The Rights of Man'. Paine annihilated Burke's defence of the French court, summed up in the famous phrase: 'He pities the plumage, but forgets the dying bird'. The book was published in 1791, but by 1794 it had sold over 200,000 copies and probably eventually reached the sale of a million. In 1791 a poor London cobbler, Thomas Hardy, had formed a workers' group which met in local taverns. Then, on 25 January 1792, they founded the London Corresponding Society, with just eight members at the beginning, and dues of one penny a week. Groups were formed in Sheffield and other parts of the country. This was the first attempt of the working class in any country, in a fumbling fashion it is true, to organise itself into a political association.

Thus, one effect of the French revolution, of enormous historical importance, was to provoke the first faltering steps of the British industrial workers to organise themselves politically. The Stockport club declared 'By our labour are the monarchy, the aristocracy, and the clergy supported . . . We are not the swinish multitude described by Mr. Burke'. Club delegates at a meeting in Norwich in March 1791, called for all 'friends of liberty' to form a general union. This was interpreted by the British aristocracy as an attempt to emulate the French Convention.

The bourgeois closed ranks as the revolution threatened the foundations of their rule. The Whigs split, with the majority supporting the king and Pitt in a counter-revolutionary crusade against the revolution. The handful of Whig sympathisers of the revolution, such as Fox and Wilberforce, were isolated.

The bourgeois clamoured for persecution of the democrats. Pitt took active steps to persecute the British 'Jacobins' and the democratic reform societies. The repression was more intense in Scotland than elsewhere. Reactionary bourgeois voluntary associations, involving so-called 'watch committees', and the search for 'subversive' pamphlets and placards, were encouraged by the government. The judiciary dispensed fines, the pillory and prison. Juries were packed in Scotland, prompting Fox to declare, 'God help the people who have such judges'. The word of an agent provocateur was usually all that was required for the democrats to be found guilty. All propaganda on behalf of reform was considered to be seditious. The repression in Scotland was greater because the movement was more widespread and bolder there than in England itself. Muir was arrested just as he was about to leave for France. Together with Pastor Palmer of Dundee, these martyrs were sentenced to fourteen years transportation to Australia. Their crime had been to collaborate in organising a Scottish Convention of 35 societies in which York, London and Ireland were represented.

Despite the repression, juries did not always carry out the stipulations of the judges or the government. Thus, Hardy and others were arrested but were freed after a famous trial. The Republicans were further strengthened by the rise in unemployment and poor harvests in 1794-95 which resulted in riots in London, Birmingham and Dundee. In the rural areas, Justices of the Peace were threatened by the hungry population. The army itself became infected and executions for insubordination were introduced.

The crisis came to a head in October 1795 just when Parliament was opening. A huge meeting was held on 27 October 1795, where both the king and Prime Minister Pitt were insulted by rioters. This led to a wave of repression, the outlawing of all 'seditious assemblies and publications' and the bill which prohibited assemblies of more than 50 persons unless a declaration and the presence of a magistrate had been obtained beforehand. Huge protest meetings took place, and there was talk of an insurrection to overthrow the government, but this came to nothing. Feeling the ground tremble beneath their feet, the British bourgeoisie combined this repression with concessions including a kind of 'minimum wage' at the employers' expense and a cost of living index of articles essential for a worker. The radical movement therefore gradually subsided and lay dormant for a further 15 years.

However, it partially re-appeared in the mutinies at Spithead and the Nore in 1797, which arose from the brutal discipline, foul food and low wages of the seamen. In Ireland, the revolution had the greatest impact. It stimulated the movement for national independence and a huge agrarian revolt against the Anglo-Irish landlords of the land hungry Irish peasantry. The first attempt of French troops to assist in an Irish uprising against the British in 1796-7 was abortive. The second attempt was made in the spring of 1798, but it met with defeat, and the government rounded up the leaders before they could leave for France. The peasant rebellion broke out in June before the French had arrived and was ruthlessly repressed. When General Humbert's fleet landed in Ireland in September, it was too late.

In the face of the threat of the French revolution, the British bourgeoisie used sectarianism on a mass scale for the first time. It was in this period that the Orange Order was organised by the British ruling class as a means of reinforcing sectarian divisions and of repressing the predominantly Catholic population. It was to serve the British ruling class as a valuable weapon in the next century and a half. Yet the revolution endured—and its effects are felt even now.

Re-writing history

The French ruling class, who rest on the foundations created by the revolution, have spared no effort to celebrate its 200th anniversary in July 1989. Millions of people thronged the streets of Paris to commemorate the fall of the Bastille on 14 July. Mugs, keyrings and all kinds of trinkets have flooded France. Plays, TV and radio programmes by the hundred, with raging debates as to the origins of the revolution, have combined with 800 'new' books to push the events of 1789 to the fore. Why then produce another book which seeks to 'rake over the coals' of events which have been covered again and again? The answer to this question is to be partly found in the unfamiliarity of the present generation of workers with the sweep and impact of the mighty events of 200 years ago.

The *Independent* commented that a third of French people interviewed in an opinion poll were unable to record a single important social change introduced by the revolution. Things stand no better, if anything a lot worse, in Britain and other capitalist countries. Nor is this an accident. As the brutal mouthpiece of British capitalism, *The Economist*, put it: 'who controls the past greatly influences the present'. Therefore, the great majority of historians are engaged in a giant exercise in obscurantism and dust blowing. Under an avalanche of so-called 'facts', right-wing historians have sought to bury the enormous significance, the processes and particularly the role of the masses in the revolution.

A 'good' or a 'bad' revolution?

Led by Francois Furet, a modern renegade from socialism, they 'seek to distinguish a *good* revolution (1789) from a *bad* one (1793-4)' (*Economist* 24 December 1988). Despite the plaudits heaped on him by the bourgeois press, Furet is not at all original. Plekhanov, father of Russian Marxism, gave a finished explanation of the bourgeois historians' views of revolution 100 years ago. He explained that the British capitalists take entirely different views of the revolution of the 1640s, which created the conditions for the spectacular growth in its system and power, and that of 1688. The first they describe as 'a great rebellion' and the second as 'a glorious revolution'. In the first revolution, the plebeian masses—a term used to describe the unemployed, the artisans, small shopkeepers, comprising varying social classes—played a decisive role, while in 1688 they intervened hardly at all. In France, however, the process was reversed.

First came the 'glorious revolution' of 1789 and only later on in 1793-4 the 'great rebellion'. In fact, even in 1789 the revolt of the Parisian masses was decisive. However, the difference between this, the first revolution, and the second revolution of 1793-4 was that the Parisian masses formed the backbone of the dictatorship of the Jacobins—the radical wing of the French revolutionary bourgeoisie. This was manifested partially through the controlled economy, which began to encroach on the rights of the bourgeoisie. Of course, in the final analysis, given the undeveloped level of the productive forces, and therefore of the working class, all that Jacobinism amounted to was, in the words of Karl Marx, 'nothing but a plebeian way of settling accounts with the enemies of the bourgeoisie, with absolutism, feudalism and philistinism'. Yet, despite the historic debt which the French and the European bourgeoisie owed to the Jacobins, this did not prevent them—both at the time and subsequently—from resorting to one calumny upon another against their leaders and against the heroic sans-culottes—the Paris poor, literally, those without trousers!

What the Bolsheviks were to the ruling classes of the twentieth century, the Jacobins and sans-culottes were to the ruling classes of the eighteenth. To Edmund Burke, chief propagandist of the counter-revolution of the time, they were 'a band of rogues and cruel assassins, reeking with blood'. To Taine, ex-liberal of 1848 and terrified by the 1871 Paris Commune, they were 'vagabonds, tatterdemalions, many almost naked, and most armed like savages, of a terrifying physiognomy, they are "the kind one does not recall having met in broad daylight".'

Even to Thomas Carlyle, a romantic torn between admiration for the sans-culottes and horror at their alleged anarchy, they were 'an enraged National Tiger' for 'Victorious anarchy'.

Contrast this with Lenin who, on the eve of the Russian revolution, could write:

> Bourgeois historians see Jacobinism as a low point. Proletarian histo-
> rians see Jacobinism as one of the highest peaks in the emancipation
> struggle of an oppressed class. The Jacobins gave France the best
> models of a democratic revolution and of a resistance to a coalition
> of monarchs against a republic. The Jacobins were not destined to
> win complete victory, chiefly because eighteenth century France was
> surrounded on the continent by much too backward countries, and
> because France herself lacked the material basis for socialism, there
> being no banks, no capitalist syndicates, no machine industry and no
> railways . . . .
>   It is natural for the bourgeoisie to hate Jacobinism. It is natural
> for the petit bourgeoisie to dread it. The class conscious workers and
> working people generally put their trust in the transfer of power to
> the revolutionary, oppressed class, for that is the essence of Jacobin-
> ism, the only way out of the present crisis, and the only remedy for
> economic dislocation and the war.

Yet it is not merely to defend the historical reputation of Jacobinism that the present generation needs to familiarise itself with the events of the French revolution and reexamine them.

This was a bourgeois, not a socialist, revolution. The sans-culottes were not a movement of the industrial working class as some have claimed. The proletariat at that stage was largely undifferentiated from the journeymen and small masters. Nevertheless, the germ of the modern labour movement, as with the Levellers in the English revolution, is to be found in the movement of sans-culottism.

Above all, a study of the revolution, of the processes particularly between 1789 and 1796, is important also for understanding the revolutions which have characterised the twentieth century. Just as officers in a capitalist army cannot restrict themselves to the study of modern wars—in the military academies they ponder even the lessons of the battles of ancient Rome and Greece—no more can the modern generation of socialist and Marxist workers merely restrict themselves to the twentieth century. Indeed Marx, Engels, Lenin and Trotsky worked out the laws of revolution and counter-revolution on the basis of an assiduous study of the French revolution. All the general features and stages of the French revolution are contained in their works.

The best of conscientious modern historical researchers thoroughly bear out their analysis. But these are now unfortunately in a minority, besieged by a growing band of right-wing historians. For every work of Georges Lefebvre, the giant historian of the French revolution, and the able modern works of those like George Rudé, there are a hundred which seek to bury the real lessons of the French revolution under an avalanche of lies and distortions. It is our task to reaffirm the real lessons of the French revolution. In so doing we can show the indissoluble link between the struggle of the masses of Paris in the last decade of the eighteenth century and the modern working class movement.

Is the French revolution over?

The French revolution left its indelible imprint on French society right up to the present. It has been the benchmark for left and right, polarised for the last two hundred years into two bitterly divided camps. Bourgeois historians wish to bury once and for all the French revolution. Like many before him Furet has declared 'The revolution is over'. Reformist historians, on the other hand, have come largely to the same conclusion. Edgar Faure, for instance, at one time appointed by socialist President Mitterrand to direct the official commission preparing for the bicentennial celebrations, stated shortly before his death: 'It is necessary now to achieve a reconciliation . . . to put the idea of doing away with right-left confrontation, which transforms France into two seemingly inpenetrable blocs.' He also stated 'Today we are living in an open society, a society based on law. The revolutionary break is no longer necessary.'

The bourgeois historians would agree with the reformists, not just in relation to the present but also in relation to the past. French society in the eighteenth century, they argue, was doing nicely and needed just touching up here and there to fit it out for modern development. 'Reforms' on the pattern of the 1688 British 'Glorious revolution', the installation of a constitutional monarchy, was all that was required in the France of the late eighteenth century.

In combatting the idea of revolution 200 years ago, they wish to put paid to the concept of revolution today. Yet, a conscientious examination of French society of the period will prove that all the conditions for revolution existed in 1789.

Jacobin leader Camille Desmoulins

Background to revolution

THE POPULATION of France in 1789 stood at roughly twenty-five million. Despite recent attempts to prettify the reign of the 'enlightened despot' Louis XVI, the great mass of the French people lived in grinding poverty and backwardness. Eighty per cent of the population lived in the rural areas, with the mass of the peasants eking out an existence on small plots of land barely able to support them and their families.

Society was rigidly divided into three orders: the nobility, the clergy and the Third Estate—which combined the urban population, the peasants *and* the bourgeoisie. The nobility numbered an estimated 400,000, with 4,000 noble courtiers, a kind of 'leprous court camarilla', at the top of the aristocratic pyramid. There were an estimated 100,000 priests, nuns and monks but, as Abbé Sieyèes pointed out, the clergy did not constitute a homogeneous 'class', but was more a 'profession'. It was divided on class lines between the bishops—'nobles of the church'—and the ordinary priests and nuns. The lower clergy, close to the people, could not fail to reflect the growing class hatred for the nobility including their own bishops. This was reflected in the movement of the ordinary priests over to the side of the Third Estate during the Estates General—the meeting of all three orders together—which was critical in disintegrating the opposition of the nobility and monarchy to the Third Estate's demands.

The hierarchy of the church owned at least one-fifth of the land of France. Together with the nobles and buttressed by the power of the monarch, they were the dominant force in French society. As many commentators have pointed out, they lived in the most ostentatious luxury,—'squandermania' on a vast scale—and viewed with aristocratic contempt the mass of the population of France. This mass was crushed by all manner of feudal and semi-feudal restrictions, with one tax piled upon another.

The French peasant paid a tithe to the church; *taille, vingtième, capitation* (a poll tax) and *gabelle* (salt tax) to the state; and to the 'seigneur' (lord) of his parish, whether lay or ecclesiastical, he paid a varying toll of obligations, services and payments ranging from the *corvée* (forced labour exacted in cash or kind) and the *cens* (feudal rent in cash) to the *champart* (rent in kind) and *lods et ventes* (a charge on the transfer of property). In addition to this, if he did not own the land outright he would have to pay for the use of his lord's mill, wine press and bakery.

Feudalism . . . or not?

Unbelievably, some bourgeois historians, led by the British historian Alfred Cobban, have argued in a completely hair-splitting, scholastic fashion that France could not be described as 'feudal' on the eve of the revolution. They point to the disappearance of serfdom in most regions of France: therefore a revolution to overthrow 'feudalism' was entirely unnecessary. A little bit of 'social engineering', a heavy dose of the famous British 'compromise' between the aristocracy with the rising bourgeoisie could have guaranteed French society a far more peaceful and less sanguinary evolution. The revolution was therefore an unfortunate 'misunderstanding' between the contending classes, particularly the aristocracy and the 'bourgeoisie' in French society. Cobban's 'pure' feudalism is as much a fiction as is a 'pure' capitalism. Every social system contains within it exceptions to the general rule and also the seeds of its own destruction. Different and antagonistic forms of production and classes co-exist alongside the predominant form. Economically, feudalism in its 'pure' form can be reduced to individual production by unfree peasants, serfs, and individual appropriation of the surplus produce of the peasant by the lord of the manor. The superstructure built on this is the military fief (peasants forced to do military service at the whim of their feudal master), the feudal state etc.

Capitalism is a system of social production, workers producing in common in big industry, etc, and the individual appropriation of the surplus they create through their labour by the capitalist. Within the womb of capitalism develops the working class, with its own organisations, parties, unions, co-operatives etc, the embryo of the future socialist society. Property relations, the ownership of industry by a parasitic handful of private owners, comes into conflict with the increasingly 'socialised' productive forms. This contradiction can only be overcome on the basis of changing 'property relations'—transferring ownership of industry to the state now collectively managed and controlled by the working class. Long before its overthrow, feudalism had ceased to exist in the schematic form envisaged by Cobban. Even at its height, alongside unfree serfs there was always a residue of free peasants. Serfdom had largely disappeared in Britain by the fourteenth century.

In France, the unfree peasants' labour service was gradually changed into money payment. Moreover, the guilds and chartered towns came into being as exemptions from feudal vassalage and obligations. With them developed the bourgeoisie, who bought fiefs—rights over certain land and the peasants on it—in France as early as the thirteenth century. Feudalism in its 'pure' form was undermined moreover by the growth of the absolute monarchy which extended its power at the expense of feudal seigneurs, by promoting royal tax collection, sale of offices etc.

Absolutism, although in the final analysis resting on the feudal nobility, was not averse to leaning on the bourgeoisie against the aristocracy. What remained therefore of feudalism by the seventeenth century? In Cobban's 'pure' form very little. But as Rudé has pointed out: 'Of its "bastards" or offshoots a considerable amount'. These included the previously mentioned taxes. Above all, the old manorial system was not only maintained but reinforced in the latter half of the seventeenth century.

On the eve of the revolution, *mainmort* was imposed on half a million peasants; the peasant was forced to reside on the lord's estate, he was restricted in his right to bequeath land and even to marry, had to take enforced oaths of allegiance etc. At the same time the peasants were still expected to make payments in kind to the manorial lord and sometimes to do *corvée*. On top of this came the 'feudal reaction' (the peasants in France did not quibble about terms like Cobban) in the latter half of the seventeenth century. Taxes were increased on an already crushed rural population and new 'lords' re-examined the manorial rolls through an army of special agents, in order to increase the return on their investments. Francois 'Gracchus' Babeuf, the legendary leader and inspiration for the communist 'Conspiracy of Equals', to be dealt with later on, started out as such an agent. His experience of what these exactions meant for the peasants combined with the sweep of the revolution pushed him in the direction of communism.

The aristocracy

The aristocracy was a closed and largely hereditary caste. The restrictions and tolls imposed on commerce and industry were an impediment to the development of the bourgeois who counterposed 'freedom' of trade and competition to the 'restrictions' of feudalism. The French aristocracy clung tenaciously to its privileges. Thus, whereas in the earlier part of the eighteenth century under Louis XlV, some bourgeois were promoted to high office, no such hopes could be entertained by the bourgeois under Louis XVl. The aristocracy had a monopoly in the army, church and state. Several of the 'parlements', the councils of the nobility, were refusing to admit 'commoners' into their ranks. Moreover, an ordinance in 1781 made it impossible for a bourgeois to qualify as an officer candidate in the army unless actually rising from the ranks.

Thomas Carlyle summed up the aristocracy:

> Close viewed, their industry and function is that of dressing gracefully and eating sumptuously. As for their debauchery and depravity, it is perhaps unexampled since the era of Tiberius and Commodus . . . Such are the shepherds of the people: and now how fares it with the flock? With the flock, as is inevitable, it fares ill, and ever worse. They are not tended, they are only regularly shorn. They are sent for, to do statute-labour, to pay statute-taxes; to fatten battlefields (named 'Bed of Honour') with their bodies, in quarrels which are not theirs; their hand and toil is in every possession of man; but for themselves they have little or no possession. Untaught, uncomforted, unfed; to pine dully in thick obscuration, in squalid destitution and obstruction: this is the lot of the millions.

Consequently, between 1750 and 1785 there were 100 peasant uprisings. It is true these did not take the form of the peasant jacqueries, the rural rebellions that swept the countryside in previous centuries, but were largely disturbances in the main market towns. They were mainly provoked by rising food prices in years of shortages. The last of these outbreaks took place in May 1775. Some historians have nevertheless concluded that, rather than deprivation, rising rural prosperity characterised the period immediately before the revolution. Therefore the revolt of the 'lower orders' was entirely unjustified. As we shall see, it was precisely the betterment in the conditions of at least a layer of the rural population, followed by a worsening in their conditions immediately before the revolution, which was a trigger for the events of 1789 itself.

The urban masses

It was not just the peasantry but the urban masses who also suffered. Between 1730 and 1789 wages in France rose by more than 20 per cent, but grain prices increased by 60 per cent! Strikes and industrial disputes were a feature of France throughout the eighteenth century, including the Lyons silk weavers' strikes and bloody riots in 1744, 1779 and 1788, and the strikes of bookbinders, building workers, carpenters, farriers, locksmiths and others between 1776 and 1789.

Crashing at every turn against the fetters imposed upon them by feudalism, the Third Estate, that is twenty-four and a half million out of the twenty-five million population of France, was in a state of open rebellion on the eve of the revolution.

Marxism has pointed out that war is often the midwife of revolution. The French autocracy had expended not a little of its treasure in supporting the revolt of the American colonists against its age old enemy Britain, 'perfidious Albion'. This was to have two calamitous consequences for the French monarchy. The state was bankrupted and the example of the American revolution which invoked the 'Rights of Man' proved contagious for France itself.

The soil upon which these ideas took root had been ploughed up by the great French philosophers of the eighteenth century. 'The wind always blows the tops of the trees first': intellectual ferment and criticism of the old order are an inevitable preparatory stage for revolution, as is strikingly obvious in the case of the French revolution. Engels pointed out that:

> The great men, who in France prepared men's minds for the coming revolution, were themselves extreme revolutionists. They recognised no external authority of any kind. Religion, natural science, society, political institutions were all subjected to the most unsparing criticism: everything had to justify its existence before the judgement seat of reason—or give up existence.

France had not experienced a Reformation and the church, as we have seen, was a pillar of feudalism. It was naturally subjected to withering criticism, as with Voltaire's savage satires. But this criticism was not restricted to religion alone. All scientific tradition and political institutions were subjected to scrutiny and criticism. Materialism, which had been the preserve of a handful of 'cultivated men' in Britain, was seized on in France as a revolutionary weapon against the autocracy. Rousseau declared in the opening words of his famous *Social Contract*: 'Man is born free, and everywhere he is in chains'. The philosophers, with their appeal to 'eternal reason', idealised the demands of the rising bourgeoisie. Of course, the philosophers advanced the cause of the whole of the Third Estate in their criticisms of unequal taxation and manorial rights. Yet in the words of Lefebvre: 'They rendered particular service to the bourgeoisie . . . who like all classes striving for supremacy saw themselves as the champion of the whole "nation" against "despotism".'

However, as Engels again points out: 'The French revolution had realised this rational society and government. But the new order of things, rational enough as compared with earlier conditions, turned out to be by no means absolutely rational'. Nevertheless the philosophers provided the intellectual armoury for the revolutionary classes to forge the weapons for the overthrow of the old society.

At the end of the American war in 1783, the state could only make up the colossal deficit accumulated during the war by further borrowing. Such a policy could not continue indefinitely. Therefore Calonne, the king's minister, proposed increased taxation to fill the gap.

King against nobles

The drop in the purchasing power of the masses and the already colossal tax burden carried by them meant that little more could be extracted from this quarter. Calonne therefore proposed to tax the nobles. This was linked with a threat to the 'manorial rights' of the church, and a proposal to give responsibility for apportioning taxes to provincial assemblies elected by landowners without distinction as to order. This mild measure of 'reform' was to meet the same kind of fate as similar earlier attempts of Turgot and Necker. Both had been frustrated in their attempts to introduce very mild fiscal and other reforms which merely trimmed the finger nails of the aristocracy.

The aristocracy therefore came into collision not just with Calonne, but with his master Louis XVl. It was Karl Marx who pointed out that 'revolution always starts from the top'. Feeling the ground trembling beneath their feet, one section of the ruling classes urges reforms in order to prevent revolution from below. Another section, clinging tenaciously to the old order, advocates further repression.

In the case of the French revolution it was the tussle between the monarchy and the nobility in defence of their respective rights and privileges which opened the floodgates. This conflict was to set in motion a movement which would destroy both. Chateaubriand later lamented: 'The patricians began the revolution—the plebeians finished it'. The major problem for Calonne was that the monarchy had become completely discredited. Indifferent to the suffering of the masses, Louis was devoted to the hunt, drank and ate to excess and was the laughing stock of his courtiers. The Queen, Marie Antoinette, had gained a reputation of a Messalina, the dissolute wife of Roman emperor Claudius, and had lost face in the 'Diamond Necklace Affair' of 1785. She had attracted the hatred of the masses for her gambling, lavish clothes, obtaining lucrative positions for her friends, etc. The 'Diamond Necklace Affair' involved a complicated swindle, whereby the court jeweller was duped into handing over a fabulously expensive diamond necklace, valued at 1,600,000 francs, to a woman impersonating Marie Antoinette. This led to a trial and the imprisonment of the conspirators. But, during the trial, Marie was vilified, condemned as 'that Austrian bitch', and booed and hissed by the crowds. The Paris police wrote to the Queen, suggesting that she should stay away from the capital for fear of provoking riots! Moreover, it was rumoured that most of her children were not the king's!

An American, on the eve of the overthrow of the monarchy, commented about Louis: 'What will you have from a creature who, situated as he is, eats and drinks and sleeps well, and laughs and is as merry a grig as lives'. Another commented: 'Usually he listened, smiled and rarely decided upon anything. His first word was usually no'.

Louis' diary completely bears this out. For the early part of July 1789, it reads: 'Tuesday 7th: Stag hunt at Port Royal, killed two. Wednesday 8th: nothing. Thursday 9th: nothing. Deputation of the Estates General'. As the storm clouds gather, as a social earthquake gives warning tremors, this vacuous king writes: 'Friday 10th: nothing. Replied to the deputation of the Estates. Saturday 11th: nothing. Departure of M Necker. Sunday 12th: Vespers and *salut*.' On the eve of the storming of the Bastille, his diary records: 'Monday 13th: nothing.' And the entry on 14 July, as Louis' world was turning upside down, with the capital convulsed by revolution? The diary records: 'Tuesday 14th: nothing'!!

Trotsky points out that the French monarchy, like the Romanov monarchy a hundred and thirty years later, went toward the abyss 'with the crown pushed down over their eyes'. Comparing the French king and the Russian tsar, he pointed out that both were 'moral castrates, who are absolutely deprived of imagination and creative force . . . they had just enough brains to feel their own triviality, and they cherished an envious hostility towards everything gifted and significant'. The king was therefore a very unreliable prop for Calonne in his conflict with the nobles. He was soon forced out, to be replaced by Brienne. The latter, compelled to follow the same course as Calonne, also offered to retain the three orders in the provincial assemblies, thus maintaining the privileged power of the aristocracy, and to leave the clergy's manorial rights alone.

However, the nobles replied that it was not within their power to consent to taxes. Prompted by Lafayette, a noble who had played an important role during the American revolution, they hinted that only the Estates General, which had not been convened since 1614, had this power. Brienne submitted his proposals to the Paris parlement, but this body refused to register the decree on the land tax and demanded once more that the Estates General be convened to deal with the matter. The decrees were however promulgated on 18 November 1787. The Duc d'Orléans protested, and the king retaliated by exiling the Duke and two councillors. The parlement came to their defence and, in order to ward off attack, published a declaration of 'fundamental laws', stating that the right to raise taxes belonged to the Estates General and that no Frenchman could be arbitrarily arrested or detained. They also defended the 'customs and privileges' of the provinces. Louis retaliated by abrogating to the Royal tribunals rights which the nobles and seigneurs exercised previously through the manorial court. This in turn triggered off a revolt of the provincial parlements and the clergy. This was paralleled by riots which broke out in Paris and several other cities. In the 'day of tiles', the citizens of Grenoble rose on 7 June 1788 to shower troops with tiles from the roof tops.

Convening the Estates General

Checked at every turn, Brienne and the king yielded and conceded that the Estates General should convene on 1 May 1789. But Brienne was forced to resign on 24 August 1788. The king recalled Necker, who immediately reconvened the parlement of Paris that had been suspended by the king. This body in turn declared that the Estates General would consist of three orders as in 1614. Each would have the same number of representatives but would meet separately and would have a veto over the others. As Lefebvre pointed out: 'The nobility and clergy were made masters of the assembly. This was the aristocrats' victory'.

However, the precedents set by the nobles were noted by the spokesmen of the Third Estate. They would use similar methods against the nobles as the latter had used against the monarchy. The mere announcement of the convening of the Estates General had a profound effect on the whole of the Third Estate. One section of the bourgeois had favoured the revolt of the aristocracy, whereas others were largely indifferent. But all of that was changed by the convening of the Estates General. The tradesmen of Paris, the journeymen and apprentices, were already in revolt at the dramatic upward movement in the price of bread. The country-side was astir with rebellion. A peasant woman had declared to the English traveller, Arthur Young, a few days before the fall of the Bastille: 'Something was to be done by some great folk for such poor ones.' She did not know how this was to be done or by whom. 'God send us better, for the taille and manorial rights are crushing us'.

All the oppressed classes in French society were roused to their feet by the mere convocation of the Estates General. The bourgeoisie finally hoped that the nobles would concede 'equal rights'. Their hopes however were to be cruelly dashed by the decision of the Paris parlement to uphold precedent in the Estates General. This involved separate voting by orders, thus guaranteeing a majority in the Estates General to the nobles and the clergy.

The fury of the Third Estate, particularly the spokesmen of the bourgeoisie, exploded. Notwithstanding the ideal schemes of 'reform' which today's historians put forward at the safe distance of two hundred years later, their 1789 predecessors declared war on the aristocracy. The latter refused to grant any concessions which touched on their fundamental interests. Barnave, a spokesman for the Third Estate, had written earlier: 'The roads are blocked at every access'. Abbé Sieyès, then canon of Chartres, lamented that he would never obtain the office of bishop. Lefebvre comments: 'Since the doors were everywhere closed, the only course was to break them down.' To advance its cause, the bourgeoisie of France, in contrast with that of England and the United States, was led to emphasise the equality of rights. It was forced to champion the rights of all oppressed classes. Sieyès summed this up when he declared 'What is the Third Estate? Everything. What has it hitherto been in our form of government? Nothing. What does it demand? To become something'. At the same time he vented his hatred of the nobility: 'This class is assuredly foreign to the nation because of its do-nothing idleness'. Mirabeau, an impoverished ex-noble, turning to ancient Rome for inspiration, praised Marius, 'for having exterminated the aristocracy and the nobility in Rome'.

The upper bourgeoisie, in preparation for the Estates General, organised itself into the 'patriot' party. Their activities were co-ordinated through the 'committee of thirty' which included not just bourgeois but also sections of the liberal nobility such as Lafayette. This has led some bourgeois historians to conclude that the French revolution was not at all a bourgeois revolution. After all, sections of the nobility such as the Marquis de Lafayette played a prominent role in the revolution itself. With the breakdown of feudalism, some sections of the nobility, through impoverishment, were forced into the ranks of the Third Estate. Even some wealthy aristocrats, under the impact of the American revolution and the blind alley which feudal society meant for France, had gone over to the side of the bourgeoisie.

The overwhelming majority of the nobility were, however, implacably opposed to any reforms. They had entered the struggle as a champion of the 'people' against the monarchy. But now the king, outraged by the 'disloyalty' of the nobles, under the prompting of Necker decided to allow double representation to the Third Estate. This would allow it to outvote the privileged orders. As Rudé comments: 'the aristocracy and parlements, so recently the acclaimed custodians of the nation's "liberties" against ministerial oppression, [now] appeared as its bitterest enemy.' The nobility warned the monarchy 'The state is in danger . . . a revolution of governmental principles is brewing . . . already the suppression of feudal rights has been proposed . . . Could Your Majesty resolve to sacrifice, to humiliate, his brave, his ancient, his respectable nobility? . . . Let the Third Estate cease attacking the rights of the first two orders'.

Nor was the struggle restricted to words alone. In some of the provinces the nobles violently protested at the doubling of the vote of the Third Estate. In Brittany, class struggle broke out into open civil war. In Rennes, fights broke out at the end of January 1789. Meanwhile the masses in both the urban and rural areas were driven to revolt by the sudden deterioration in their conditions. The roots of this lay in the crisis in agriculture. As a result of France's entry into the American war, there was a recession in which prices fell both in industrial and farm products but particularly in wines and textiles. After 1778 the prices in the wine market fell by fifty per cent. They rose a little in 1781 because of scarcity but not enough to compensate the peasants who, in practically every area of France, relied on vine growing as the most profitable crop. Grain prices also fell and the peasants' misery was compounded by the drought of 1785 which killed off livestock.

This general crisis in agriculture merged with the economic catastrophe of 1787-89. From agriculture it spread to industry with huge increases in unemployment in Paris, Lille, Lyons, Troyes, Sedan, Rouen and Rheims. The failure of the grain crops in 1788-89 steadily pushed up the price of bread. Urban craftsmen and workers were drawn together with the peasants in common hostility to the government, landlords, merchants and speculators. Some bourgeois historians still maintain that the general prosperity of France, evident throughout the last half of the eighteenth century, was increasing at the time of the revolution. They conclude that the deterioration in the conditions of the lives of the masses could be discounted as a factor in the revolution. It is true that France had doubled her income throughout the seventeenth century. Yet a big part of the increased income from the colonial trade was re-exported. A general rise in prices moreover, which had benefitted the large landowners and bourgeoisie, completely outstripped the rise in wages. Reserves were so low that bad harvests inevitably meant famine in the countryside as the peasants were affected both as producers and consumers. Moreover, the massive increase in food prices in 1787-89 meant that the masses' expenditure on bread shot up to half, three-quarters and even four-fifths of their earnings.

Revolutionary change

The existence of relatively recent prosperity, rather than staving off the threat of revolution, only stoked up the fires. It is neither economic upswing nor a downswing which in and of itself, provokes revolution. It is the change from one period to another which creates the conditions for a rapid change in the consciousness of the masses, their receptiveness to revolutionary ideas and to a revolutionary rupture in society. Such were the conditions that were maturing amongst the masses in the period 1788-1789 in France.

The mood of the masses was decisive in ensuring the victory of the revolution of 1789. They acted not just in defence of the bourgeois dominated National Assembly in its conflict with the king and nobility, but saw in a revolutionary change the means whereby they would transform their own miserable conditions. It was these masses, the heroic sans-culottes, who were to be the driving force of the French revolution itself. While compelled to lean on these masses to destroy feudalism, the French bourgeois feared them. The liberal bourgeoisie in 1789-96 were to display the same fear of the plebeian masses of Paris as the German and Russian bourgeoisie were to later show towards the industrial working class.

Trotsky in his theory of the permanent revolution showed that, in the modern epoch, the liberal bourgeoisie is incapable of carrying through the tasks of the capitalist revolution: that is, land reform, unification of the country and freedom from imperialist domination. Through its investment in the land and the landlords' investment in industry, it is enmeshed in the perpetuation of feudal and semi-feudal land relations. Moreover, confronted by the modern proletariat, it is terrified of leading a mass movement which will inevitably go beyond the framework of bourgeois society. It is for these reasons that Trotsky concluded that the bourgeois democratic revolution could only be carried out not *with* but *against* the liberal bourgeoisie. It is only the working class, even though numerically small in a backward country, which can mobilise the peasantry to carry through the bourgeois democratic revolution. This movement, having taken power, would in turn 'grow over' to the socialist revolution on a national and international scale. This fear of the bourgeoisie of a mass movement to carry through the bourgeois democratic revolution was commented on by Marx during the 1848 revolution. The cowardly German bourgeoisie stopped halfway in its struggle against feudal Junker reaction. It feared the proletariat more than it did feudal reaction. In the light of the experiences of the 1848 revolution Marx coined his famous phrase about the 'permanent revolution'.

The French bourgeoisie displayed the same fear of the 'lower orders' as its German and Russian counterparts, and as the present colonial and semi-colonial bourgeoisie do today. Engels, commenting 100 years after the great revolution wrote:

> The bourgeois, here (France) as everywhere else, were too cowardly to defend their own interests . . . .from the day of the Bastille on, the people had to do all their work for them . . . .without their intervention on 14 July, 5-6 October, until 10 August and 2 September etc the bourgeoisie would have fallen each time before the old regime . . . .the Coalition in league with the court would have crushed the revolution, and that consequently these plebeians (the sans-culottes) alone carried through the revolution.

The French bourgeoisie *did*, however, preside over the carrying through of their revolution. Their representatives, at least the most extreme wing, *did* form an uneasy alliance with the plebeian masses to smash feudalism. Their descendants in the backward countries today, as with the Russian bourgeoisie in 1917, however, are incapable of emulating them.

Why the difference in the attitude of the bourgeoisie today and in 1789? The explanation is to be found in the fact that the bourgeoisie today confronts an entirely different situation than that obtaining in 1789. Then, industry, even in the most developed countries, such as Britain, was subordinate to agriculture, which was the main source of wealth and still dominated economic relations. Concentrations of workers in some large enterprises did exist, but it was the small business, with the master and a handful of workers, which predominated. This absence of large scale industry, the weakness of the productive forces—science, technique and the organisation of production—and consequently of a proletariat meant that socialism was impossible at that stage. The socialist transformation of society is only possible after capitalism has exhausted *all* possibilities of further growth. This was clearly not the case in France, or of any other country in 1789. The capitalists had a long road ahead of them in developing industry, society and thereby the working class.

The force of circumstances, in the shape of ferocious feudal reaction, compelled the bourgeoisie to go to the extreme of leaning on the Jacobins and the sans-culottes. They were not, however, confronted by a powerful working class, as they were later, or as the Russian capitalists faced in 1917. The triumph of plebeian petit bourgeois democracy could only be a temporary episode, which would clear the way for the development of capitalism, and thereby the political rule of capital.

Nevertheless, the French bourgeoisie, even at its birth, displayed that fear of the 'lower orders' which would become full blown later, when confronted with a powerful proletariat, organised and disciplined by the very development of capitalism itself. Therefore the *elements* of Trotsky's theory of permanent revolution, both from the standpoint of the bourgeoisie – fear and hesitation in the face of the mass movement—and from that of the masses themselves—pressure to go further, etc—were already present in the French revolution.

Following the Paris Commune of 1871, the French bourgeoisie, terrified at the emergence of a powerful proletariat, deliberately held back the development of industry—and thereby the development of the working class.

Rentier capital—banking, exploitation of colonial possessions and investment abroad—predominated over industrial capital. One of the effects of this was that French capital invested heavily in Russia—alongside British capitalism—which in turn developed industry and the mighty Russian working class. Thus, dialectically, the very power of the French workers contributed indirectly to the emergence of the Russian workers, the force which led and carried through the Russian revolution.

Thus, while attempting to bend the movement of the sans-culottes to its will, the French bourgeoisie at the same time viewed it with dread.

The Réveillon riots

In the period leading up to 1789 the masses, particularly those in Paris, showed their mettle in a series of movements. Most of these took the form of protests at the scarcity and the price of food. Yet in

April 1789 the so-called 'Réveillon riots' took place in the Faubourg Saint-Antoine (the various parts of Paris were called the *faubourgs*; they had once been suburbs, but had been incorporated into the city). These riots were remarkable in the history of the revolution for two reasons. They took place in the area which was destined to become famous as the stronghold of sans-culottism during the revolution itself. It was at the same time one of the few insurrectionary movements distinctly of wage-earners. The movement was triggered off by the remarks of Réveillon, a wallpaper manufacturer employing 350 workers in his factory in Faubourg Saint-Antoine. On 23 April he made a speech in which he complained about the high costs of production and the burden imposed on industry by the high level of wages. Outraged, 600 workers gathered near the Bastille to hang an effigy of Réveillon. In the succeeding days, protests and demonstrations, involving thousands of workers, climaxed in the storming of Réveillon's house.

Gardes francaises—army reservists—protecting the house opened fire and a massacre followed. The masses fought back with cries of 'Freedom . . . we will not be moved' while others shouted 'Long live the Third Estate'. The irony was that Réveillon was himself a prominent member of the Third Estate. Yet even in this movement, the masses were picking up the slogans of the revolutionary bourgeoisie in its struggle against the privileged orders and using them to advance their own demands and interests.

The Estates General meets

In the provinces, peasants were already stopping food convoys, raiding markets and destroying game reserves. It was against this background of sharpening crisis that the elections and meeting of the Estates General took place. When it met in May everything was done to humiliate the Third Estate. Its representatives were ordered to wear the traditional black (in contrast to the splendid attire of the aristocrats) and enter the meeting hall by a side door. At the outset of the meeting, an incident involving the king and the Third Estate took place. When the king had seated himself and put on his hat, the privileged orders put theirs on likewise. The Third Estate, in defiance of the usual custom, imitated them, but when Louis XVI saw what was happening, he again bared his head so that all hats had to be quickly removed. This 'war of the hats' was a precursor of a more violent exchange between the different orders that was to take place in the succeeding period.

The bourgeoisie had placed high hopes in the Estates General.

While the king had agreed to double representation for the Third Estate, he was opposed to the demand that the three estates should meet in common. They were invited instead to meet in separate assemblies. The bourgeoisie felt cheated because, even with 'double representation', they could still be outvoted by the other two orders. The Third Estate therefore refused to meet separately and invited the other orders to join them. The nobles and the bishops resisted, with the bishops having great difficulty in restraining the parish priests (who outnumbered them by five to one) from joining their 'fellow commoners'.

The period between the meeting of the Estates General and the July revolution was essentially a period of deadlock between the Third Estate on the one side and the privileged orders on the other. To begin with, the spokesmen of the bourgeoisie appealed to a section of the privileged orders, particularly the clergy, 'in the name of the god of peace' as Mirabeau put it, to come over to their side. The noble orders, however, frustrated all attempts to compromise. The bourgeois deputies were also under the ferocious pressure of the masses, who were looking towards the Estates General as a solution to their problems: 'All France is in a roar' wrote Carlyle later.

Aristocratic intransigence was connected in the consciousness of the masses with a plot to drive up the price of food, to create famine conditions in order to shipwreck all attempts at reform. As we have seen, the price of food had increased sharply in 1789. A worker commented to an observer that the 'princes had cornered the grain market on purpose so that they could the more easily succeed in toppling M. Necker, whom they all had so great an interest in overturning'. This was one manifestation of the 'great fear' which lay deep in the psyche of the rural and urban masses of France and which was to play a significant role in the revolution. Lefebvre has demonstrated that it was connected in the minds of the masses with the issue of food supplies, always precarious at the best of times. The French peasants had a deep fear of 'brigands'. Starving, roving bands of ex-peasants, landless labourers and discharged servicemen, sometimes did indeed pillage the fields of the peasants, particularly in periods of famine. Invariably the peasants connected this with the exactions inflicted on them by the nobles. The urban masses had the same fear of food hoarders which they invariably ascribed to the privileged orders and their agents in the towns and cities.

This phenomenon of the 'great fear' was to be a recurring theme throughout the revolution. It was not, as royalist historians have asserted, either an invention of the revolutionaries or a blind inchoate movement of the masses without any material foundation. In the charged atmosphere of revolution and counter-revolution it was not difficult for the masses, with their age-old fear of 'brigands', to ascribe, with full justification, the same motives to the nobles and international feudal reaction. Of course, there were sometimes excesses, such as prison massacres, but even these were rooted in the attempt of feudal reaction to smash the revolution by force of arms. The mass movement was worked up into a frenzy at the spectacle of the aristocracy's attempt, during the Estates General, to sabotage all their hopes and aspirations.

The whole of France followed the deliberations of the Estates General. The news was carried by a thousand different channels to the masses. Hundreds of pamphlets were produced and new journals mushroomed. The masses were mobilised by journals such as *Les Révolutions de Paris*, published by Loustalot, which bore the motto 'The great appear great in our eyes only because we are on our knees. Let us rise'.

Although largely illiterate, the masses were able to follow events as the speeches of the deputies of the Third Estate in the Estates General were often read out publicly to mass meetings gathered outside town halls throughout France. Moreover, the journeyman, the small businessman, was usually able to read and communicated the news to his workers. Under the constant pressure of the masses the representatives of the Third Estate at Versailles decided to act.

The National Assembly

At the beginning of June, Sieyès declared that the moment had come for 'cutting the cable'. It was proposed that the privileged orders should be summoned to meet together with the Third Estate. If they refused, a roll call should be taken of all those who were present and those not in attendance should be declared 'defaulted'. The Third Estate should then declare itself 'the national representatives of the people,' if necessary without the king's consent. A few parish priests joined them and on 16 June they declared themselves the 'National Assembly'. Three days later, the deputies were, it seems by accident, locked out of the usual meeting place and were forced to meet in the neighbouring indoor tennis court. It was there that they took the famous 'Tennis Court Oath' in which they declared:

> That all members of this Assembly shall at once take a solemn oath never to separate but to meet in any place that circumstances may require, until the constitution of the kingdom shall be laid and

established in secure foundations; and that after the swearing of
the oath each and every member shall confirm this indefeasible
resolution by signing with his own hand.

Only one deputy refused to take the oath. At a royal session on 23
June, however, Louis declared that the acts of the Third Estate were
null and void but authorised 'joint deliberations and vote by head
in affairs of general interest'. However, defending the privileged
orders until the end, he expressly excluded any re-consideration of
the 'ancient and constitutional rights of the three orders, the form
and consititution of future Estates General, feudal and manorial
property, and honorific privileges and useful rights of the first two
orders'. He also defended the rights of the clergy in all religious
matters. In a warning to the Third Estate he declared: 'If you do
not obey, then I shall send you back home and alone I shall create
the happiness of my people'.

The nobility greeted the king's defence of their privileges with
wild enthusiasm. When the nobility withdrew from the Estates
General, the Third Estate remained in position with Bailly, one of
their representatives, declaring: 'The nation when assembled cannot
be given orders'. At first the king was disposed to forcibly disperse
the assembly but then declared: 'Oh well, the devil with it—let
them stay'. More importantly, the Parisian masses now intervened,
stirred up by the rumour that Necker, who was supporting the
claims of the Third Estate, was about to be dismissed. Soldiers
also refused to fire on the crowd and deputies of the Third Estate
gathered at Versailles. The king was forced to retreat.

On 27 June, the remnants of the other orders were instructed
by him to merge with the Third Estate in the 'National Assembly'.
However, the king was merely playing for time. Swiss and German
troops were concentrated on the outskirts of the city ready, the
king imagined, to snuff out without difficulty the resistance of
the 'National Assembly'. But he had reckoned without the rising
revolutionary temper in the capital.

The insurrection begins

PARIS WAS the key to the revolution in 1789 and the scene of its greatest dramas over the next six years. Its population at the time of the revolution has been estimated at between 524,000 and 660,000. Only London with a population of 850,000 was larger than Paris at this stage. The city contained about 10,000 clergy, 5,000 nobles and 40,000 financial, commercial, manufacturing and professional bourgeois. The rest, the great majority, were the small shopkeepers, petty traders, craftsmen, journeymen, labourers, vagrants and city poor, who formed what later became known as the sans culottes. It was also estimated that about 300,000, or half, of these were 'wage-earners'. As Rudé comments, 'In eighteenth century France, the term *ouvrier* (worker) might be applied as readily to independent craftsmen, small workshop masters—or even, on occasion, to substantial manufacturers—as to ordinary wage-earners; in its most frequent use it was synonymous with artisan'.

Although clashes, including quite bitter strikes, took place between masters and journeymen, these were of secondary importance and the wage-earner was usually more concerned with the price of food—particularly of bread—than with the amount of his earnings. This mass—the sans-culottes—played the decisive role in July 1789 and at each turn in the revolution. With the rise in the temper of the Faubourgs, the bourgeoisie decided to intervene. The Duc d'Orléans, who had gone over to the Third Estate at Versailles, set up a permanent headquarters at the Palais Royal. Orléans was the pretender, a rival for the throne of Louis. His considerable funds were used to produce pamphlets, organise orators and give direction to the growing opposition to the Capetian—Louis' family name was Capet—monarchy.

The traditional bourgeois of Paris were gathered together in the 407 electors of the Parisian Third Estate. Their headquarters were at the Hôtel de Ville—the Town or City Hall. They largely restricted themselves in the first period to paper schemes for setting up a citizens' militia, a *milice bourgeoise*. The Duc d'Orléans proved to be much more audacious. Crowds directed from his headquarters at the Palais Royal forcibly released eleven guardsmen from the Abbaye prison who had been incarcerated there for refusing to fire on the crowd at Versailles on the night of 22-23 June.

The army

Under the pressure of the masses, the royalist army itself began to disintegrate. Carlyle makes an apposite comment:

> Good is grapeshot, Messeigneurs, on one condition: that the shooter were also made of metal! But unfortunately he is made of flesh; under his buffs and bandoliers, your hired shooter has instincts, feelings, even a kind of thought. It is his kindred, bone of his bone, the same canaille that shall be whiffed; he has brothers in it, a father and mother—living on meal-husks and boiled grass . . . .If he shed Patriot blood, he shall be accursed among men. The soldier, who has seen his pay stolen . . . his blood wasted . . . and the gates of promotion shut inexorably on him if he were not born noble,—is himself not without griefs against you. Your cause is not the soldier's cause; but, as would seem, your own only, and no other god's nor man's.

Carlyle at least understood what the liberal and reformists are blind to: that the army, even one such as that of the *ancien regime*, is in general a copy of the society from which it ushers. In a pre-revolutionary or revolutionary period, the army will tend to split under the pressure of the masses. The troops will not, however, come over to the side of the masses unless the latter have demonstrated in practice that they are prepared to go the whole way. This the Parisian masses gave abundant evidence of in July 1789. They did not act primarily in defence of the Assembly. They were more concerned about their own fate, being convinced that the city was surrounded by royalist troops and that they were about to be bombarded from Montmartre and the Bastille.

On 10 July, 80 artillery men who had broken out of their barracks in the Hôtel des Invalides, a former military hospital, were feted in the Palais Royal and the Champs Elysées. Then, urged on by the queen, Louis dismissed Necker on 11 July and sent him into exile. His replacement was a nominee of the queen, the Baron de Breteuil. This ignited the tinderbox of Paris. The news reached the city on the noon of the twelfth. The masses flocked to the Palais Royal where the future Jacobin leader Camille Desmoulins, with pistol and sword in hand, called the masses to insurrection with the cry 'To arms—to arms'. Demonstrators swarmed into the boulevards and reached Saint-Honoré. The cavalry undertook to make them disperse and charged the crowd in the Place Louis XV. The *gardes francaises* (army reservists) who had gone over to the people in turn attacked the cavalry. Besenval, commander of the Parisian garrison, withdrew to the Champ de Mars. Crowds thronged the streets and emptied the debtors' jail at La Force.

Barricades were going up, trenches were being dug to repel the cavalry and paving stones were carried to the upper floors of the five- and six-storey buildings that dominated the narrow streets. The capital was now in effect in the hands of the people. The tocsin (the bell) summoned the Parisian masses to battle. The hated *barrières* (customs posts) which were resented by shopkeepers, wine merchants and small consumers, because they drove up the price of consumer goods, were burnt down. The arsonists were concerned also to destroy the monopoly of the *Fermiers General* (the tax collectors) and above all to control the exit and entry of persons and arms in and out of the city. Fearing bloody revenge from royalist troops, the main concern of the masses was for arms. Thus a frantic search for arms took place throughout the city. The bourgeois were alarmed at this mass movement. Earlier, one of the deputies of the Third Estate, a bourgeois from Bar-le-duc, Duquesnoy, summed up the attitude of the bourgeoisie when he wrote: 'One must work for the good of the people, but the people must do nothing for it themselves'. Now that the people were acting for themselves and moreover with arms in hand, the alarm bells began to ring. Carlyle once more describes the scene: 'On Monday the huge City has awoke, not to its weekday industry: to what a different one! The working man has become a fighting man; has one want only: that of arms. The industry of all crafts has paused;—except it be the smith's, fiercely hammering pikes; and, in a faint degree, the kitchener's, cooking offhand victuals'. A detachment of civilians and gardes-francaises broke into the monastery of Saint-Lazare, searched it for arms, released prisoners and removed food to the central market. Everywhere there was a search for arms. Religious houses, gunsmiths, armourers and harness makers were raided in different parts of the capital.

The bourgeoisie now took decisive measures in order to attempt to control the situation. They organised, with the permission of the king of course, a national guard. It was composed of 'men of property', who formed the backbone of this force. All vagrants and homeless persons and even a large part of wage-earners were excluded. It was in the words of Barnave, spokesman for the bourgeoisie, to be 'bonne bourgeois'. Yet the arming of the masses went much further and wider than the bourgeois National Guard. Following the attack on the Invalides, the masses now concentrated on the Bastille.

Storming the Bastille

Royalist slanderers, contemptuous of the 'ignorant' Parisian masses, have always pictured the assault on the Bastille as something of a damp squib. The impression has been given that the Bastille was stormed in order to release revolutionaries incarcerated in this royalist stronghold. In fact it held at the time of the July insurrection no more than seven prisoners. It was of course a hated symbol of royalist despotism. But the main reason for storming the Bastille was in order to capture the arms which, it was believed, were stockpiled in large numbers within its confines. Moreover, the guns of the Bastille could have wreaked havoc if they were turned on the Parisian masses, particularly in the Rue Saint-Antoine, the main bastion of the revolution. The storming of the Bastille has been told many times and does not need to be repeated in detail here.

However, the crowds which besieged the Bastille did not in the first instance intend to storm it. The governor, de Launey, negotiated with a deputation from the bourgeois 'electors' for the handing over of gunpowder and arms. The besieging crowds filled the outer courtyard and the governor, mistakenly believing that an assault was about to take place, ordered his men to fire. The besiegers lost 98 dead and 73 wounded. The bourgeois 'electors' lost control of the situation and detachments of gardes-francaises and armed civilians from Saint-Antoine and the neighbouring districts used cannons against the main gates. Such was the outrage at de Launey's unprovoked attack on the crowd earlier, that he, together with six other defenders, were massacred. This was the culmination of an insurrectionary movement which resulted in the complete capitulation of the monarch and the disintegration of the court party. Its effects reverberated throughout the whole of France and beyond its borders.

Trotsky once commented that only a minority directly participates in an insurrection, but the strength of that minority lies in the support or at least sympathy of the majority. It was not just those who directly participated in the storming of the Bastille who 'made' the revolution of 1789. They had the support of the overwhelming majority of the Parisian masses. This can be gauged by the fact that it is estimated that a quarter of a million Parisians, the vast majority of them opposed to the privileged orders and the monarchy, were under arms at this stage.

The court camarilla urged the king to flee and seek support in the provinces. They themselves fled into foreign exile. The king, like Archimedes, was seeking a point of support with which to shift the axis of his changing world. His problem was that this did not exist. As one of his marshals put it: 'We can get to Metz alright, but what are we to do when we have got there?'. The problem for the monarchy and the aristocracy was that the movement in Paris was echoed in the provinces and to some extent paralleled it. The dismissal of Necker also provoked an immediate reaction there.

In some towns the arsenal was broken into and workers' militias were set up. The governor of Dijon was arrested and nobles and priests were confined to their dwellings. At Rennes the garrison deserted to the side of the people and the military commander fled. At Caen, a similar movement seized the citadel and attacked the hated *tribunal de sel* (the court which enforced the salt tax).

At Le Havre, the naval arsenal was seized and in Bordeaux insurgents took control and fraternized with the troops. As in Paris the commanders of the royal troops showed little enthusiasm for fighting for the dying regime. At the same time, the bourgeoisie of the provinces aped their counterparts in Paris. They set up 'safe' militias restricted to 'men of property'. The 'municipal revolution' spread to the whole of France. It differed from place to place but in all instances it refused to recognise the royal power and only obeyed orders from the National Assembly.

Central authority was weakened and in the vacuum which was created 'towns started to conclude mutual assistance pacts, spontaneously transforming France into a federation of Communes'. The Paris Commune—which was again to rise in revolution in 1871—was in 1789 at first firmly under the control of the bourgeoisie, was the model for the bourgeoisie throughout France. Of course, the masses went much further than the bourgeoisie wished. In Paris, the assembled citizens met in the districts—divisions established for elections to the Estates General—claiming to supervise the municipal authority which had been set up to replace the 'electors'. This was the beginning of the 'direct democracy' which the sans-culottes cherished and fought for in the course of the revolution.

The peasant rising

The movement of the peasantry ran alongside that of the urban masses. It is a myth that the peasants tamely waited for the deliberations of the bourgeois National Assembly, soon to become the Consitituent Assembly, for the satisfaction of their demands. Nowhere, as Trotsky commented was feudalism abolished without force or the mobilisation of the masses.

The fundamental axis of the French revolution was in fact a plebeian movement in the towns, supplemented by a peasant war to destroy the remnants of feudalism. It was only through the establishment of the Jacobin petit bourgeois democracy in Paris and the other towns of France that the feudal yoke was lifted from the backs of the peasants. They found a leadership in the towns, without which the peasant movement could not have succeeded. Indeed, the peasants supported the urban petit bourgeois democracy—the Jacobin/sans-culottes alliance—only up to the liquidation of feudalism in 1793. Thereafter, peasant hostility to the towns provided a reservoir for Thermidorean, and later Bonapartist, reaction.

In the months before and after the July revolution the countryside experienced huge rural insurrections, grain riots, assaults on millers, granaries and food convoys: 'A vast national conflagration against the *régime féodal* as a whole and, in particular, against manorial registers housed by the landlords in the chateaux, monasteries or abbeys'.

In the previous year, peasants had protested at the game laws, hunting rights, royal taxes, tithes and seigneurial dues. News of the Paris insurrection stimulated this movement even more. The agricultural crisis had increased the number of vagrants in the country areas as well as intensifying the hostility of the peasants to the landlords. The peasants concluded that the aristocrats together with the brigands were about to avenge themselves on them. They armed themselves, but when the brigands did not arrive they turned their arms against the mansions of the landlords instead. Burning chateaux lit up the skyline from one end of France to another. The target of this peasant war was not so much the buildings of the landlords themselves, but the manorial rolls through which the landlords had exacted further tribute from the peasants. This mass movement was decisive in forcing the hand of the bourgeoisie who dominated the National Assembly.

Under its pressure, the Assembly declared on the night of 4 August 1789 that 'The feudal regime had been utterly destroyed'. In fact it had not, at least not yet. The remnants of serfdom were abolished, along with the *corvée* and ecclesiastical tithes. However, some of the more oppressive privileges and obligations—the *cens, quit rent, champart, lods et ventes* among them, were made 'redeemable': that is, the peasants had to pay for them by cash payment. But the masses went way beyond the letter of the law.

In all revolutions, the august bourgeois representatives in their assemblies invariably have to scramble to keep up with the insurgent masses. Thus, in the Spanish revolution, the Republican government elected in February 1936 managed to get round to 'legally' freeing workers who had been imprisoned in 1934 following the suppression of the Asturian commune only in September 1936 two months after Franco's seizure of power! The masses, however, had already torn open the jails and released them as soon as the victory of the 'Popular Front' was announced!

The 'redemptions' of the National Assembly imposed on the peasants amounted to an expected total compensation of four thousand livres. This however remained a dead letter. The peasants simply refused to pay and the Jacobin Convention ratified the accomplished fact by a decree of July 1793, declaring the outstanding debt null and void.

The poverty and privations of the masses were the spur which drove the revolution forward. A survey by the Constituent Assembly in 1790 showed that some ten million people out of a population of twenty-five million were in need of relief and three million were considered to be 'paupers'—ie beggars!

In the aftermath of the storming of the Bastille, the king hesitated between flight and passive resistance until such time as the necessary forces could be assembled to crush the revolution and restore the rights of the aristocracy and the monarchy. He chose the latter course. On 17 July he made the journey from Versailles to the outskirts of Paris escorted by 50 deputies (Robespierre among them). He donned the new revolutionary cockade of red, white and blue, as a token of his acquiescence.

Flushed with confidence, the bourgeoisie proceeded to lay down the principles of its regime. These were enshrined in the famous 'Declaration of the Rights of Man' which began with the words: 'Men are born and remain free and equal in rights'. Wordsworth summed up the ardour which the declaration and the revolution aroused in all opponents of despotism. He wrote in the famous words from his poem *Prelude*: 'Bliss was it in that dawn to be alive, but to be young was very heaven'. Conversely, feudal reaction foamed at the mouth at the events unfolding in France.

The Rights of Man were defined as 'Liberty, property, security and resistance to oppression'. It also sanctioned the right to rebellion. While it is a general statement of universal principles and human rights, it was in essence in favour of the revolutionary bourgeoisie and those from the clergy and liberal aristocracy who had come over to their side. As Rudé has commented: 'Running through it all is the concern of the nation's new rulers that the system to be devised must be adequately protected against the triple danger of royal "despotism", aristocratic privilege and popular "licentiousness".'

Though the declaration had proclaimed the right of all citizens to representation and involvement in the making of laws, it did not specify who should have the right to vote or how it should be exercised. This allowed Sieyès, consummate representative of the bourgeoisie, to propose that only those of 'substance and property' should be allowed to vote in two electoral stages. Thus the population were divided into the 'actives' and 'passives', with the 'actives' alone having the right to vote.

Under the 1791 Constitution formulated on the basis of the declaration, only 50 per cent of the population could qualify as electors in the 'primary' assemblies, and only one in a hundred might qualify as a national deputy. This of course was far more democratic than elections to the unreformed British Parliament, but the masses who had made the revolution were denied the 'legal' right to vote. Nevertheless, it was the intervention of these masses which was to push the revolution forward and to shatter the schemes of a section of the bourgeoisie to establish a 'constitutional monarchy' on the British pattern.

The bourgeoisie entertained fond hopes that the king would acquiesce in the establishment of such a regime. In August 1789, the liberal nobles, in conjunction with an estimated half of the deputies of the Third Estate, dubbed the 'monarchiens', controlled the Assembly. They wished to establish in France a bicameral system of an upper and lower house with the right of veto still retained by the king. They were denounced by the other patriots as 'Anglomaniacs', or simply 'Englishmen', for wanting to establish the English system in France. The majority of the patriots, however, still considered that the king should be given a 'suspensive' veto: that is, the right to delay legislation for three sessions but not an 'absolute' veto.

The king, while treacherously pretending publicly to accept the revolution, secretly wrote to one of his supporters on 5 August: 'I will never consent to the spoliation of my clergy or my nobility. I will not sanction decrees by which they are despoiled'. In the teeth of royal intransigence, the bourgeois in the assembly were once more impotent. Using the divisions in the ranks of the patriots the king blocked all attempts to 'legally' complete the destruction of feudalism. It would take a second dose of revolution and the removal of the king from Versailles to Paris to bring the monarchy to heel.

The masses, particularly the starving population of neighbouring Paris, looked on the manoeuvres of the king and the monarchists

revolution towards the French wife of King Charles I and also by the Russian workers and peasants towards the German wife of the last of the Romanovs, Tsar Nicholas II. Paris, when it learnt of the banquet, construed this as preparations for an assault on the assembly. Marat advised that forces be concentrated at the Hôtel de Ville in order to ward off the royalist counter-revolution. The district assemblies went into permanent session and, on Danton's initiative, the Cordeliers Club demanded prosecution for the crime of *lèse-nation*—a crime against the nation, as opposed to *lèse-majesté*, a crime against the king—of anyone wearing any but the tricolour cockade. The women of Paris were particularly stirred up at the debauchery at Versailles, the sumptuous living and the arrogance of Marie Antoinette.

The march on Versailles

On the morning of 5 October, a revolt began in the central markets and the Faubourg Saint-Antoine. The women led this movement in both areas. In the market the movement was started by a small girl, who set out from the district of Saint-Eustache beating a drum and declaiming against the scarcity of bread. Meanwhile, in the Faubourg Saint Antoine, the tocsin was rung at the instigation of the women calling the citizens to arms. The women from both areas then converged on the Hôtel de Ville. As well as demanding bread, they demanded arms for their men for the march on Versailles.

During the invasion of the Hôtel de Ville, despite the presence of three and a half million livres in cash and the near starvation of the assailants, not a penny was taken. Indeed, at all stages of the revolution, the sans-culottes never resorted to looting but in fact punished any such manifestation, sometimes with death. Lafayette and Bailly were missing from the Hôtel de Ville and therefore the women, numbering about 7000, put at their head Maillard, one of the combatants of 14 July, and proceeded to march to Versailles. As they marched they chanted 'Let us fetch the baker, the baker's wife and the little baker's lad'. Thus the Parisian masses, particularly the women, at this stage identified the king—the baker—and his return to the capital as a guarantee of plentiful food supplies. Lafayette, who was the commander of the bourgeois National Guard, first of all argued against emulating the women. But the whole of the city rang to the cries of 'To Versailles'.

Threatened with the *lanterne* (that is, being hung from the nearest lamppost!), he consented to lead 20,000 men composed of National

Guardsmen and about a thousand sans-culottes on a march to Versailles. Meanwhile Louis XVI, weighed down by the affairs of state, had gone hunting as was his custom in critical moments.

The women reached Versailles at five-thirty in the evening and a clash took place between the guards at the palace and the Parisians. Some of the demonstrators entered the king's chateau and penetrated even as far as the ante-chamber of the queen's apartment. One of the guards from a window shot dead a cabinet-maker from Saint-Antoine. Enraged, the crowd slaughtered two of the guards and cut off their heads.

Lafayette's forces arrived at Versailles at ten that night and Lafayette himself was cordially received by the king. However, the masses were clamouring for the return of the king to Paris. One bourgeois commented that they were complaining that they had lost a day's wages in the march to Versailles and 'If the king did not come to Paris, and if the bodyguard were not killed, Lafayette's head should be stuck on the end of a pike'. One of the leaders of the crowd, in language which could be readily understood by the masses, declared: 'You don't see that you are being screwed by Lafayette and the king. The whole damn bunch has to be taken to Paris'.

The king was under the impression that the only issue at stake was his veto over the constitutional decrees of the Assembly. Under mass pressure, and as a means of disarming the movement, he accepted the constitutional decrees of August and September and therefore the power of the Assembly. As Lefebvre comments: 'The Assembly adjourned at 3 am. It alone had gained a substantial advantage from the day's events, for the king had "accepted" the constitutional decrees and implicitly recognised that his "sanction" was not needed. Once again, a mass movement had assured the success of a juridical revolution'. The king considered that this was the end of the matter but the Parisian masses were determined to bring him back to the capital. The king appeared on a balcony with the royal family and the masses roared 'To Paris'. After a few minutes the king accepted. Both the royal family and the National Assembly, the latter after a vote, agreed to transfer to Paris.   The October days were a turning point in the revolution. The revolutionary bourgeoisie wished to defeat the plots of the king and the aristocracy to frustrate and roll back the gains of the July revolution. The people of Paris were no less concerned at this conspiracy but were also motivated by their desperate social and economic situation. They combined together in the October days to weaken the veto of the king, with real power from now on lodged in the Assembly. The masses contributed the lion's share to the victory in October but the bourgeoisie once more reaped most of the benefits. Having leaned on the people to gain victory over the aristocracy and 'despotism', the bourgeoisie now wanted them to go quietly back to sleep. The masses however had other ideas. The day after the king returned to Paris crowds of women invaded the corn market and dumped rotten flour into the river. This was followed in late October by a baker, Francois, receiving summary justice through the *lanterne*.

Dual power

The Assembly, in an attempt to quell the mass movement, introduced the death penalty for rebellion, and also censorship aimed at the radical press, such as Marat's paper. The bourgeoisie, eager to consolidate its power, did not hesitate to trample underfoot one of the proclaimed aims of the revolution: 'liberty'. A Bastille labourer, Michel Adrien, was publicly hanged on 21 October, a bare four months after the revolution, for allegedly attempting to provoke 'sedition' in the Faubourg Saint-Antoine. Similar measures were taken against the peasants. The bourgeois National Assembly also took measures to curb any movement of the workers. However, neither the monarchy nor the aristocracy had abandoned all hope of rolling back the revolution.

A situation of dual power, a stage which is seen in all great revolutions, both of the bourgeois and of the socialist type, obtained in France at this stage. The Assembly, the backbone of which was the upper levels of the Third Estate, concentrated the real power in its hands. However, it had not fully succeeded in removing the prerogatives of the king. Louis had sent secret messages to Vienna and Madrid repudiating all the concessions he had made since 15 July. Aristocrats began to flood out of France and the 'monarchiens' in the Assembly withdrew, some of them in an attempt to raise the provinces against Paris. Over 300 deputies asked for their passports, a clear sign that they were intending to flee, but in the event only 26 actually withdrew from the Assembly.

The king still hoped that enough internal reserves existed, bolstered by the threat of foreign intervention which in time could be used to organise the counter-revolution. The phenomenon of dual power or 'double sovereignty' would be manifested in subsequent stages of the revolution but involving different forces. This first period of dual power between the Assembly and the monarchy comes to an end with the flight of the king to Varennes in June 1791.

In its early days, the Assembly, in conjunction with the Commune, took energetic measures on the food front. Regular supplies of grain were supplied to the bakers. The bourgeoisie set about organising its regime, administration, economy and army. Latterday right-wing bourgeois historians have laboured to 'prove' that the French revolution was of little economic consequence. Thus *Newsweek* (20 February 1989) declared: 'One of the most persistent misconceptions about the revolution is the idea that it "modernised" a backward, under industrialised France.' It points to a growth in industry thoughout the eighteenth century but then declares 'The revolution slowed these processes'. It further cites the views of an 'expert', Pierre Chaunu, a right-wing professor at the Sorbonne University. He declaims that the revolution worked to the advantage of France's main rival. 'It [the revolution] made England the industrial power of the nineteenth century'. These merely echo similar arguments deployed by the bourgeois historians against the historical legitimacy of the Russian revolution. According to this school of thought, the Russian revolution, by inaugurating a planned economy, actually retarded rather than enormously speeded up the Russian economy. It is an incontestable historical fact, that no economy in history, not even the Japanese economy at the height of the post-war boom, has equalled that of Russia since 1917. The colossal potential of the planned economy, despite the enormous wastage and mismanagements, inevitable in a totalitarian one party regime, is justified in the advances of the Russian economy and in the living standards of the Russian masses. As to the argument that France would have progressed at an even greater rate, a cursory examination of the fact proves otherwise. The unification of the national market was carried through. Domestic traffic was freed from the tolls and the check-points. This in turn provided the framework for the future untrammelled development of the productive forces. Lefebvre comments:

> Unbinding its fetters was not enough to transform production, and for that reason many have stated that the revolution did not mark a decisive date in French economic history. In fact, it neither launched nor accelerated production, and later the war actually retarded it. The Constituent Assembly nevertheless paved the way for future events. We have no better testimony to the advent of the bourgeoisie than the first proclamation of economic freedom in Europe.

The bourgeoisie were, of course, not prepared to extend the same kind of 'freedom' to the incipient proletariat. The assembly closed down the public workshops which had been set up in 1789 to absorb the unemployed. At the same time, they introduced the infamous Le Chapelier law making combinations illegal. That is, they out-lawed workers coming together to oppose the massive increases in food prices or to fight for wage increases. This measure had been preceded by strikes of carpenters and other workers and was intro-duced at the behest of the manufacturers. Not a single deputy, not even Robespierre, objected to the introduction of this law. Trade unions were outlawed throughout the revolution, and the law was not finally repealed until 1884.

However, the year 1790 was better than most for the mass of the French population. The price of bread had fallen to 8 sous per pound by June of 1790. This together with other factors was responsible for a peaceful interlude in the revolution. This period of relative social peace lasted with minor interruptions until the spring of 1791.

The tempo at which a revolution develops is determined by a number of factors. A critical element is undoubtedly the role of the revolutionary party — what Marxists call the subjective factor — in the revolution. Thus, the Russian revolution developed in a rapid fashion, over nine months, primarily because of the role of the Bolshevik Party, with a far-sighted revolutionary leadership, which was in place *before* the revolution.

The French revolution gave power to the Jacobins only after a period of almost four years. The Jacobin party, for that is what it was, did not exist prior to 1789, but was created in the fire of events themselves.

In a revolution, which is a process not just one act, such pauses are inevitable. The masses after the exertions of an insurrection pause and take stock. However the National Assembly, subject to the ferocious and conflicting forces after the October days, could not arrive at agreement on any fundamental issue. The deputies were under the constant scrutiny of the Parisian masses who, from the time of the Estates General, had flooded out the visitors galleries, sat in gangways and sometimes on the chairman's and speakers' rostrums. They never hesitated to boo and hiss at speakers who aroused their ire. There were constant interruptions, the hearing of *cahiers* (petitions on grievances) from 'hordes of delegations which filed up to the speakers' desk facing the president'.

The constitutional monarchists, now led by Lafayette, attempted to draw sections of the patriots over to their side with the offer of ministerial positions. Mirabeau proposed that the king should be allowed to select ministers as in the British 'parliamentary' system. The patriots, realising that this would split their ranks, prohibited deputies from accepting ministerial positions. Mirabeau constantly and secretly conspired with the king and the queen behind the backs of the Assembly. He even urged the monarchy to organise their own party, with him of course in the leadership. But, the Assembly was compelled under mass pressure to ratify the dismantling of the feudal system. This it achieved in a series of decrees. Thus on 7 November 1789, the 'social orders' ceased to exist and on 28 February 1790 'venality in office' was abolished from the army, which meant that 'commoners' could be promoted from the ranks. In February 1790 each commune elected a municipal council and 'manorial authority' over the villages was destroyed. One consequence of this decentralisation was a disastrous financial crisis. Having made the revolution, arms in hand, the masses refused to pay indirect taxes and were reluctant to pay any others.

The land was the main source of wealth and therefore the main source of taxation. The Assembly also taxed income and 'moveable' property, but without a proper survey taxes could not be equalised and therefore the total amount was estimated on the basis of the old 'tax system'. This particularly irritated the peasants, who, were crushed by the taxations of the *ancien regime*—the old order of feudal France. Karl Marx once commented that when the French peasants thought of the devil they imagined him in the guise of a tax collector!

The sale of Church property

The financial situation went from bad to worse. Faced with economic catastrophe, the Constituent Assembly was compelled to take emergency measures. It solved the problem by proposing the sale of church property. It used these assets as security for the issuing of 'assignats'; state credit notes which eventually became the currency of the revolution. The bourgeoisie had long looked hungrily towards the wealth of the church. The value of its properties, including those of the parishes and monastic orders, yielding an income of 100 million livres a year, represented something between 40 and 50 per cent of the landed wealth in every province of the realm. It was, moreover, exempted from taxation other than what it voluntarily ceded to the state.

With the church discredited and divided, on 2 November 1789, its estates were 'put at the nation's disposal'. In a series of other decrees the regular clergy was suppressed apart from the teaching or charity orders and they were relieved of authority to administer property. At the same time, the state set up a budget of 'public worship' and in May 1790 outlined the specific terms of sale of church land. It ordered creditors to accept payment in assignats, as a means of establishing its new currency.

These measures did not immediately bring the church into conflict with the revolution. Many of the parish priests, now state officials, were being paid more generously than before. Moreover, the Assembly had no intention of disestablishing the Catholic Church. While it recognised a fuller freedom of right to worship, extending this to Protestants (and later to Jews), it still upheld the privileged position of the Catholic Church as the state church of France. The re-organisation of dioceses as a means of saving money to the state did provoke, however, some opposition in depriving bishops and some priests of their livelihood. The refusal of the assembly, however, to submit the civil constitution of the clergy in 1790 to a vote of a synod of the church for its approval or otherwise provoked a furious opposition.

After a period of negotiation, during which the bishops of France appealed to the Pope, the assembly finally implemented unilaterally the constitution of 1790. They ordered clerics holding office to take an oath of allegiance to the constitution of the kingdom (and, therefore by implication, to the civil constitution of the clergy) yet only two of the Assembly's 44 bishops and a mere one-third of its clerical members complied. Those who took the oath were 'jurors' and those who refused were 'non-jurors'. After much hesitation the Pope came to the support of the 'non-jurors' instructing all members of the clergy to withdraw their support for the church settlement. This was an important factor in the revolution, identifying the opponents of the civil constitution as enemies of the revolution itself. The majority of the clergy were to play a counter-revolutionary role and were to earn the hatred of the revolutionaries, receiving no mercy. The role of the clergy in supporting the counterrevolution led to the ferocious suppression of the Vendée and other attempts at civil war by the aristocracy.

The counter-revolution organises

The open forces of the counter-revolution, organised behind the 'blacks'—the most reactionary wing of the aristocracy—continued even after October to organise resistance against the Assembly. They attempted to use the parlements and whipped up the provinces, particularly in the Dauphiné and Cambrésis. They also organised the suppression of the peasant movement, sometimes continuing the old 'manorial rights' in defiance of the law. In age old fashion they sought to convince the poor that only the well being of the privileged orders could guarantee the general well-being of society. If the privileged classes were ruined, the poor would also be dragged down.

Some of the aristocrats fled abroad in preparation for foreign intervention. Others openly campaigned within the borders of France for intervention, while others fomented civil war in the region of the Midi. The first conspiracy, the Languedoc plan, resulted in bloody fights in May and June 1790. This was followed in July by the Lyons plan, with a proposal for different aristocratic armies to march on the city. The insurrection was fixed for 10 December and was supposed to coincide with the flight of the king from Paris. However, a number of conspirators were arrested and the nest of aristocratic conspirators in Lyons was cleared out.

The revolutionary societies

The masses were on constant alert, encouraged by those like Marat who urged them to take offensive action against the aristocratic counter-revolution. The balance of forces in France at this stage was decisively in favour of the revolution. The main feature in the situation was the self-organisation of the bourgeoisie, paralleled by a similar movement amongst the masses. Thus in November 1789, the Breton club was reconstituted in Paris at a monastery owned by the Dominicans, who were popularly known as 'Jacobins'. This club, the 'Society of Friends of the Constitution', was hitherto known by the more popular name of Jacobins.

At the outset, the Jacobins had a high subscription rate of 36 livres, and 12 livres entrance fee. This indicated its predominantly petit bourgeois composition. Gradually, however, they acquired a mass base. Additional spectators' galleries were built, which allowed the Parisian masses to follow and influence the debates of the Club.

Following this, clubs sprang up in practically every town in France and affiliated to the Paris society. At the height of the revolution, the membership of the Jacobin clubs stood at over one million. The upper bourgeoisie and the liberal nobles who had gone over to them organised their own clubs, embryonic political parties, such as Lafayette's 'Brothers and Friends'.

As in all revolutions, an enormous thirst for knowledge developed amongst the masses, not just the petit bourgeois who were able to read, but the sans-culottes also. Revolutionary journals sprang up like mushrooms in the forest at the first hint of spring rains. It has been estimated that only one edition of Rousseau's famous *Social*

Contract was published before 1789. In the next ten years however, during a period of revolution and counter-revolution, ten more editions of the book were published!

It was amongst the most oppressed masses, the sans-culottes, that the thirst for ideas as a means of arming themselves for battle was the greatest. They were amazed and angry that they were pushed aside by the newly triumphant bourgeoisie. Four and a half million 'active citizens' were allowed the vote. These met in 'primary assemblies', which in turn chose the electors and they elected the deputy in the main town or a department. Three million 'passive citizens' were denied voting rights. Yet even under the old regime they had at least taken part in local assemblies.

The defection to the king of a section of the patriots aroused suspicions amongst the masses. This in turn led the 'district of Cordeliers' under the guidance of Danton and his friends to acquire support amongst the Parisian masses. They protected Marat from arrest and challenged the bourgeois leaders of the Commune.

Repression inevitably followed and the districts were dissolved in May 1790. This was immediately followed by the founding of a club, 'The Cordeliers', to protect the citizens against 'abuses of authority' and whose emblem was 'Eye of vigilance'. Its monthly subscription of only one penny made it accessible to the masses. Its plebeian style and the speeches of its orators were in sharp contrast to the lavish dinners of the 1789 Club and the rather academic oratory of the Jacobins. Later on, following the defection of the bourgeois 'Feuillants' to the king, the Cordeliers were to be linked to the Jacobins. At the same time the Abbe Fauchet opened his 'Cercle Social' in which the ideas of 'social', that is socialistic, christianity were preached. Several thousand Parisian sans-culottes regularly attended its meetings. Like Babeuf later on, Fauchet, in his newspaper *Bouche-de-Fer*, denounced private property and the inadequacy of mere political reform. He commanded the enthusiasm of the poorer citizens and the ire of the bourgeois republicans. These clubs undoubtedly played a critical role in the education of the masses in preparation for the future events.

The role of women

Women were also admitted to the Cercle Social and were able to join the new fraternal and popular societies which sprang up in 1791.

At no stage in the revolution, however, were women accorded the right to vote. And yet, they were a critical factor in the revolution and in the organisations of the revolutionary power. In order to belittle the enormous role of the women sans-culottes, bourgeois historians either extol the virtues of those such as the wife of the Gironde leader, Mme Roland, or ridicule the well-known feminists such as Claire Lacombe and Olympe de Gouges. These latter were involved with the *Sociétés des républicaines révolutionnaires*, the Parisian women's clubs. Standing on the extreme left, they began in 1793 to demonstrate in the streets, decked out in red and white striped trousers and items of military uniform, demanding entry to the Convention and the Jacobin Club. To begin with, the Jacobins welcomed these *citoyennes*, but their method of 'winning friends and influencing people' was to attack, sometimes physically, all those they did not like or who were opposed to them. The Jacobins and even many sans-culottes were repelled by them. This was reinforced by the fact that some, like Olympe de Gouges, supported the Gironde and opposed the king's execution.

But far more important was the movement from below of the militant women in the plebeian Faubourgs. Women played a key role, not just in the *journées*, but also in the basic organisations of the revolution—the general assemblies of the sections. This was particularly the case from the autumn to October 1793, when the women's clubs were banned.

Before then, however, as in all revolutions, women—amongst the most oppressed strata—were more determined than the men in demanding, and sometimes enforcing, revolutionary changes. In 1793, the women demanded the right to vote. At the time of the primary assemblies at the beginning of July 1793, women participated in the main assemblies of the societies, sometimes voting by acclamation, but not by roll-call. Women also enthusiastically accepted the Jacobin Constitution of 1793, and some voices were raised demanding the right to vote. According to Soboul:

> After the president of the Beaurepaire delegation had presented to the Convention his section's approval of the Constitution, he yielded the floor to a *citoyenne* who loudly demanded political equality . . . [she declared] 'Women . . . are not counted in the political system. We are asking you from the primary assemblies, and since the constitution rests on the rights of man, we demand the full exercise of those rights'. Thuriot . . . merely responded that the Convention would examine this demand.

Despite the 'legal' ban on women's voting rights, they did participate and vote in many of the Parisian sections in the summer of 1793. This in turn led to popular women's societies, such as the Society of the Revolutionary Republican Women, being formed, demanding the vote. Moreover, some of the male societies, such as the Society of Free Men, opened their doors to women. This pressure was maintained for equal rights for women up to the suppression of the exclusively feminist Society of Revolutionary Republicans by the Jacobins. However, the sans-culottes continued to admit women to the sections and popular societies.

The bourgeoisie, even its most extreme wing, were hostile to granting equal rights for women. The Thermidorean reaction in 1795 banned all women from 'attending' political assemblies, and ordered the arrest of those who would gather in groups of more than five. Despite their low cultural level, only amongst the organisations of the sans-culottes did the demands of women find an echo in the revolution. These organisations, the clubs and sections, ceaselessly explained the course of the revolution and the nature of the legislation passed by the assembly.

The movement and organisation of women was an indication of how the revolution had sunk deep roots into Parisian society and allowed a whole number of mass leaders to arise, to be trained and educated, who were to play a decisive role in subsequent developments. They were the organisers, together with the Jacobin leaders and the Cordeliers, of the mass movement which was to result in the establishment of the republic and the execution of the king. Before that stage was reached however, the revolution would feel the whip of the counter-revolution.

Peasants destroy the hated symbols of the nobility

Counter Revolution

DURING 1790 and 1791, reaction gathered around the figure of Lafayette. He had already stained his hands with the blood of the masses in suppressing the Nancy garrison in August 1790 and the subsequent execution of 41, predominantly Swiss, soldiers.

In conditions of revolution, the army could not fail to mirror the class divisions which were tearing the nation apart. The soldiers split into opposing groups with the majority of the officers, of noble birth, hating the revolution and all its institutions. They continually referred to the National Guard as 'blue porcelain that can't bear firing'. On the other hand, patriotic agitation was undertaken amongst the sailors and shipworkers at the naval bases. Robespierre demanded a thorough purge of the officer corps (a big section of them in any case had fled abroad) but the assembly, terrified of the reaction of Europe at such a measure, refused to act.

The 'July Days'

Lafayette's suppression of the Nancy garrison was a dress rehearsal for his bloody role in the massacre at the Champ de Mars in July of the following year (1791). The period leading up to this saw the counter-revolution gradually encroaching on the gains of the revolution with a layer of former 'revolutionaries' going over to the king and the court.

The anger of the masses was to culminate in the French revolution's equivalent of the 'July Days' during the Russian revolution. Such a stage is inevitable in all revolutions. Furious at the march of the counter-revolution, the masses decide to go out onto the streets. Such were the June days in the 1848 revolution in France and the movement in January 1919, known as the 'Spartacist Uprising', in Germany. They are inevitably defeated because only

48

a minority has reached the conclusion that it is necessary to over-throw the existing regime. Largely without strategy and tactics or authoritative leaders, such spontaneous outbursts of mass anger are inevitable

The period leading up to the Champ de Mars events was one of growing class antagonism not only between the people and the royal/noble conspiracy but within the representatives of the crumbling Third Estate as well. Lafayette's attempts at compromise foundered on the resistance of the aristocrats. The threat of civil war fuelled by religious divisions hung over the head of the nation.

The disappearance of feudal rights, and many other traditional institutions, to begin with resulted in increased unemployment. A big section of those unemployed were concentrated in Paris. In January, they numbered 24,000, but by June the figure had risen to 31,000. The bourgeoisie were given notice of the rising anger of the Parisian masses with the first serious breach of the peace which occurred on 28 February 1791. An attempt was made to demolish part of the Chateau de Vincennes which was being converted into an overflow prison for the capital. Patriots protested because this had been a notorious detention centre in the pre-revolutionary period. A thousand workers marched to demolish it, among whom were Bastille demolition workers. They compelled one of the leaders of the National Guard himself to lead their batallion to Vincennes, where they then proceeded to demolish the building. Lafayette scurried after them and marched back to Paris with 64 demonstrators as prisoners.

These prisoners were, however, released after huge protest demonstrations organised by the Cordeliers. Rudé comments that this event was 'but one example of the continuous efforts made by the democrats in the course of the spring and summer of 1791 to indoctrinate and to win the allegiance of the small tradesmen, craftsmen, and employed and unemployed workers of the capital'.

Their efforts were to culminate in the great demonstration on 17 July when the Parisian masses assembled to sign a petition drawn up by the Cordeliers Club, which hinted at the removal of the monarchy and the proclamation of a republic. Among those arrested in Paris during this period were large numbers of the unemployed. There were former painters, sculptors, tailors, barbers, domestic servants, jewellers, joiners and basket makers. They were constantly involved in clashes with the authorities.

Alarmed at the growth of a radicalised layer of the unemployed, the bourgeoisie, through the mayor Bailly, closed the Bastille work-shop and this was later ratified by the Assembly. The workers refused to accept the loss of their meagre subsistence allowance. They were joined by the journeymen of the Faubourg Saint-Antoine and their actions aroused the sympathy of both the Cordeliers and the Jacobin clubs. Robespierre himself, together with Camille Desmoulins, supported one such petition which demanded subsistence as a citizen's right, to be paid for out of the profits from the sale of church lands. This demonstrates, as Engels later argued, that the proletariat of Paris and the small businessmen who made up the sans culottes, encouraged by the example set by the bourgeois who helped themselves to the land of the church, were pressing forward for similar benefits for themselves. These demands comingled in some of the demonstrations with a call for the replacement of the monarchy with a republic.

The 'constitutionalists', those who supported a constitutional monarchy, denounced this movement of the Paris masses. Its newspapers condemned the popular movement which they claimed foreshadowed the dreaded 'agrarian law': that is, the distribution of property, not by 'legal' means, but by pillage and forced expropriation. Lafayette and his circle had concluded that the work of the Assembly had to be revised, property qualifications made even more stringent, the clubs to be suppressed and the press to be firmly controlled.

The bourgeoisie was in a cleft stick. To lean on the 'blacks', the royalist counter-revolution, risked unwinding the spool of revolution. They wanted a monarchy as a means of stupefying the masses and as a figurehead to be used against a popular movement. But they wished to maintain the gains of the revolution, they wanted to maintain themselves in power, giving the king larger powers and bolstered by an upper house like the British House of Lords. They wanted new elections to be called which would allow constituent members to become ministers. These proposals were defeated in the Assembly, but they had not given up hope that they would eventually realise a constitutional monarchy. However, the prop upon which they rested was suddenly knocked from under them.

The King flees

The king and his entourage decided to flee to the imperial borders. The king and queen had kept up continual contact with the royalist emigrés and the European despots who backed them. They secretly pleaded for foreign aid to overthrow the revolution. Louis even tempted the age-old enemy England in May 1791 with some 'colonial morsel' in return for 'neutrality' if an attempt to restore the monarchy should result in civil war. The Tsarina of Russia welcomed royalist emigrés enthusiastically declaring 'to destroy French anarchy is to prepare one's immortal glory'. However, at this stage, while long on words, European reaction was very short on deeds. It would take a declaration of a republic, the execution of the king and the contagious effects of a revolution throughout Europe to bring them together in military consort in an attempt to crush the revolution.

Louis and Marie Antoinette therefore decided to act on 20 June. There was plenty of evidence to indicate that the birds were about to flee the coop. Indeed there was a wide expectation of this amongst the masses. Such an enterprise could not fail to attract the attention of even the most casual observer of the actions of the court. Marat constantly warned in *L'Ami du Peuple* that the king was preparing to flee. A massive, sumptuously furnished Berlin coach was to carry Louis and his family on a secret route out of the country. His downfall was bad planning and the alertness of the masses who had been prepared for such a development by the republicans in the previous period. It was the postmaster of Sainte-Menehould, Drouet, who raised the alarm. He overtook the coach, arrived at Varennes and ordered the bridge over the River Aire to be barricaded. The king was forced to admit his identity and church bells called the peasants out.

The troops who rushed to the spot fraternised with the crowd and the king and queen were returned to Paris with threatening crowds of peasants and workers denouncing them along the way. A noble, Comte de Dampierre, who went to greet the king was murdered by a group of peasants. The news of the king's flight reached to every corner of France and once again a 'great fear' gripped the population. Nobles and priests were attacked and once more chateaux went up in flames.

The masses demanded that the king be brought back as a hostage, not as a king. The flight to Varennes completely transformed the situation in Paris. The Cordeliers declared: 'At last we are free and kingless'. The isolated voices calling for a republic rapidly increased their support. Before these events, both the Jacobins and the Cordeliers were cautious in expressing republican views. Now the Club demanded that the Assembly declare a republic or, failing that, to delay any decision until the mass of the population in the departments had been consulted.

Some of the deputies, notably Brissot, Bonneville and the Marquis de Condorcet, now came out in favour of the republic. Many of the provincial clubs did likewise. Robespierre was not foremost in this agitation, fearing that Lafayette would be installed as president in place of the king. The majority of the assembly, however, once the king had returned to Paris, set their faces against the agitation for a republic.

The upper bourgeoisie, the dominant voice in the Assembly, invented the fiction that the king had not fled but was 'kidnapped'. This despite the fact that Louis had left a proclamation behind him when he fled repudiating all the revolutionary acts of the assembly! He was obviously conspiring with the Austrian army to crush the revolution. On 24 June, the Cordeliers, massively supported by the Faubourg Saint-Antoine, launched the 'petition of the thirty-thousand' inveighing against any hasty rehabilitation of Louis. This issue resulted in deep class divisions, a bitter polarisation, in Paris and throughout the country. The Jacobin Club itself split, with the great majority of the deputies, henceforth known as 'Feuillants', defecting to form their own club. They subsequently became the bulwark of the constitutional monarchist party within the assembly. The Jacobin Club was left with only five or six deputies following this split. Its unpopularity amongst the big bourgeoisie was in inverse proportion to its growing support amongst the petit bourgeois and the Parisian proletariat—at that stage, not a homogeneous class, but composed of unemployed, shop workers, artisans and other sections. Together with the Cordeliers, they organised a massive agitational campaign throughout the capital.

However, the majority in the Assembly voted to cover-up for the king. The authorities were preparing to suppress the mass movement, and on the 16 July the Assembly, criticising the security measures of the Hôtel de Ville, instructed Mayor Bailly to take 'firm measures' to maintain order. The National Assembly was a cover for the treachery of the monarchy, as Trotsky pointed out, 'just as the Russian compromisers 126 years later were screening the treachery of the liberals'. The royalist bourgeoisie hoped to drown the mass movement in blood and settle accounts with the party of the revolution forever.

July 1917—A comparison

The republican leaders such as Robespierre did not feel strong enough to take power. Neither did the Bolsheviks in July 1917, when the revolutionary temper of the Petrograd workers was way ahead of the rest of the country, and particularly of the peasant-soldier mass. The Bolsheviks, however, put themselves at the head of the July demonstration in order to limit the damage which would inevitably result from a premature insurrection in the capital. Although July led to a temporary triumph of the counter-revolution, the tactics of the Bolsheviks ensured that the masses were educated even in the course of this 'semi-defeat'.

The French republicans such as Robespierre, in contrast to the Bolsheviks, hastened to separate themselves from the mobilisation on the Champ de Mars on July 17. Fifty-thousand had gathered in an entirely peaceful demonstration to sign a petition drawn up on the spot. It was drafted by Francois Robert and, while it was couched in radical terms, it did not specifically call for a republic. Nevertheless, its wording implied this, stating: 'To convoke a new constituent body to proceed to the replacement and organisation of a new executive power'.

The calumniators of the Parisian masses were to later argue that the demonstrators were violent. It is true that two individuals had been killed in the morning of the demonstration when they were found to be hiding under the 'altar of the fatherland'. Over 6000 had already signed the petition before the troops arrived. But Bailly, the Mayor of Paris, and Lafayette put into operation a preconceived plan to suppress the popular movement. The National Guard, numbering 10,000 and composed of the bourgeoisie, showed intense hostility towards the 'rabble'.

Massacre in the Champ de Mars

The demonstrators were mainly from the poorer sections of the Parisian population. Indeed, Rudé has demonstrated that, while the masses came from all parts of the capital, it was not just the Faubourg Saint-Antoine but previously 'peaceful and orderly' Faubourgs such as Saint-Marcel which were to the fore in the demonstration. This Faubourg was now to stand alongside Saint-Antoine as a bastion of the revolution. When a few stones were aimed at the National Guards, this was the signal to open fire. In the words of one of the demonstrators 'They fired upon the workers as if they were poultry'.

The massacre of the Parisian masses on the Champ de Mars led to a bourgeois reign of terror. Desmoulins went into hiding in Paris as did Santerre. Danton fled to England for some time and Vincent and Momoro were arrested along with many others. Marat's presses were seized and Robespierre took shelter with the carpenter Dupley. The royalist bourgeoisie was temporarily victorious but the patriotic party was irreparably split. The chasm between the two wings was signified in the spilling of blood on the Champ de Mars and the 'tricolour' terror which followed. The forces of order had murdered more men in one day than the allegedly bloodthirsty Parisian crowds had executed in the first two years of the revolution.

The majority of the bourgeois leaders gathered around the king and even sought an accommodation with the 'blacks'. The aristocrats, however, refused these overtures and the royalist bourgeoisie hesitated to make too many concessions to them. Duport, Barnave and the Lameths, masters of the assembly, frantically attempted to reach an agreement with the monarchy and to enshrine this in the 1791 constitution. However the majority of the Assembly, composed mostly of bourgeois, feared that the considerable gains accruing to them from the revolution were endangered by Barnave, who, they felt, was going too far in seeking accommodation with the right. The aristocracy for their part refused all compromises, confident that they would topple the upstart republicans on the backs of foreign armies if necessary.

The first constitution proclaimed in September 1791 was based on the Declaration of the Rights of Man, and was solidly weighted in favour of the bourgeoisie. Louis XVI, in accepting the constitution, declared 'The revolution is over'. The upper bourgeoisie which now dominated the newly elected 'Legislative Assembly' concurred. Yet this constitution was based upon a fiction, the complete independence of the legislative and executive powers. As Trotsky pointed out, it concealed a 'double sovereignty': the bourgeoisie firmly entrenched in the National Assembly, and the monarchy still relying upon the bishops, the refractory clergy, the bureaucracy, the military and, last but not least, foreign intervention. This state of affairs could only end either with the abolition of bourgeois representation by foreign intervention or, in the words of Trotsky, 'the guillotine for the king and the monarchy. Paris and Koblenz (the centre of foreign intrigues against the revolution) must measure their forces'.

The promulgation of the constitution did allow, however, for the amnesty of political prisoners. The Parisian crowd demonstrated its feelings by booing the Assembly deputies and giving a heroes' reception to Robespierre and Petion. Moreover, noble deputies profiting from their new freedom streamed across the border to join the emigré army of Prince Condé who was gathering his forces in the Rhineland.

The king in reality merely pretended to accept the constitution while continuing to intrigue with foreign feudal reaction. Hand on heart, he earnestly declared to the deputies: 'I have no longer any doubt as to the will of the people. And so I accept the constitution'. Yet Marie Antoinette had informed the Austrian ambassador that this very same constitution was 'monstrous'. She went on 'We cannot go on like this . . . our only source of help lies with the foreign powers; at whatever price they must come to our aid.' To her brother, the Austrian emperor, she wrote on the 8 September 'It is for the emperor to put an end to the disturbances of the French revolution. Compromise has become impossible. Everything has been overturned by force and force alone can repair the damage'.

On 3 December, Louis wrote to the king of Prussia personally asking for help to crush the revolution. Frederick William declined however to intervene at that stage. However, the flight of the king, notwithstanding his 'acceptance' of the 1791 constitution, had had a profound effect on his fellow European tyrants.

The Austrian emperor Leopold reacted by issuing the Padua proposals suggesting that the monarchies of Europe act in concert to save the French royal family. However, only Catherine of Russia and Gustavus of Sweden were firmly in favour of action. George III of England, prompted by the cautious Pitt, despite his touching concern for Louis, wrote that he would 'remain neutral'.

In the light of the threatening noises emanating from the courts of Europe, the 'constitutionalists', who were now ascendant in the Assembly, bent all their efforts to reconcile the monarchy with the bourgeois regime. The new Legislative Assembly was composed of 264 Feuillants with 136 Jacobins and Cordeliers, and 350 constitutionalists, half of the Assembly. And yet all efforts at compromise were dashed by the rising tide of counter-revolution throughout the country.

In August, refractory priests had provoked the peasants to rise in the Vendée. At Avignon in October 1791, they killed the mayor, and the patriots avenged his death by a massacre in the Glacière. In February 1792 they instigated uprisings in the Lozère. Levasseur, who was a deputy in the Assembly, declares in his memoirs:

> The session of the Legislative Assembly was nothing but a barely concealed war of the popular power against the royal authority . . . .this great epoch of 1791-1792 which decided France's destiny was not marked by outstanding parliamentary struggles. It was between the people and the rulers that the battle continued to be waged . . . The deputies acted as conspirators and not as deputies.

The Girondins

The Legislative Assembly saw the rise to prominence within the left of the Brissotins, named after their leader Brissot. They came to be known as the Gironde, because most of the deputies supporting them came from this area of France, although Brissot himself was a deputy from Paris. They were what Lefebvre called 'a second generation of the revolution'. They had been given their opportunity because the deputies in the previous Assembly ruled against the re-election of deputies. They were mostly petit bourgeois lawyers and writers, with a fair sprinkling of adventurers like Brissot himself. A journalist, he had led a varied life which included a period in debtor's jail in Britain, and had at one time been in the employ of the Duc d'Orléans, of the speculator Clavière and even of Lafayette.

While accepting 'political democracy', they undoubtedly saw the revolution as a means for personal advance. They moreover consorted with the business bourgeoisie—shipowners, wholesalers, bankers—who wished to defeat counter-revolution, stabilise the assignat and, as Lefebvre puts it, 'did not regard with disfavour a war that would bring lucrative contracts to suppliers'. Their support for war, however was conditional on the fact that hostilities would be confined to the continent, leaving the ports free to carry on a prosperous trade.

Marseilles, Nantes and Bordeaux were the centres of capitalism at this stage—trade and commerce being the key factors, rather than industry—and they played a decisive role in the history of the Gironde party. The Girondins made their mark in the Assembly by seeking to strike down the revolution's enemies. They also attacked the refractory, or rebellious, priests and demanded the separation of church and state.

Towards war with Austria

The Assembly did not turn their backs on those clergy who supported the revolution. They also demanded measures against the royalist emigrés and, in a decree on 29 November 1791, requested that the king summon the elector of Trier to dissolve the armed companies of emigrés assembling on his territory. They wished to turn the public against Austria and push France into a war, in the process helping to force Louis to accept patriot ministers pledged to a policy of war.

The Gironde expected that such a 'revolutionary war' would bring uprisings of the oppressed peoples in the neighbouring states. Yet the Gironde ministers would never have carried the day without the support of Lafayette and without the king doing an about face. Lafayette hoped for a short war, victory to the French armies, and with a newly acquired authority, to use the army to disperse the Assembly and crush the patriots. The king on the other hand, despairing that his fellow European rulers would come to his aid, hoped to force their hand through war. If they were attacked they would, he reckoned, come to his assistance. The Gironde 'revolutionaries' were playing into his hands. The queen even wrote to Fersen, the Swedish ambassador on December 14: 'The imbeciles! They don't even see that this serves our purpose'. Louis also secretly wrote 'Instead of civil, we will have political, war, and things will be much the better for it. France's physical and moral state renders it incapable of sustaining a semi-campaign'.

The monarchy were, in effect, proposing a policy of counter-revolutionary defeatism. Far better to be defeated and occupied by a foreign power than for the revolution to triumph. The French bourgeoisie, in its turn, was to display the same tendencies in 1871, preferring occupation by the Prussian enemy, rather than allow the triumph of the Paris Commune. In 1940 also, they preferred capitulation to the Nazi occupiers, rather than arm the French masses, thereby risking a new and much more dangerous edition of the Commune. Only Robespierre and Marat were to remain consistently and implacably opposed to the declaration of war by the Gironde dominated Assembly. Brissot convinced the Assembly that the 'patriots' in other countries were waiting with open arms for the arrival of the French revolutionary armies. Robespierre replied that the peoples of Europe would not readily welcome 'armed missionaries'. Indeed, it would allow reaction to whip up popular national resistance against the French. In addition, he believed that the French armies were unprepared and would suffer defeats. Foreseeing the schemes of the monarchists, he demanded that before opening hostilities the Assembly must weed out the counter-revolutionaries from the army and gain mastery over the king.

The revolution from the outset had an international appeal. Therefore Robespierre conceded that it may be necessary to help a revolution already underway, but he drew the line at armed intervention in other countries, including the conquest of France's 'natural frontiers'. But their voices were lost in the general clamour against the foreign enemy who harboured the emigrés.

After fruitless negotiation, France declared war on Austria on 20 April 1792, and soon faced the combined armies of the Prussians and the Austrians. Before these developments, however, under pressure from the Girondins, Narbonne, the Feuillant minister, was dismissed by the king. Dumouriez was called into office in his place. He appointed a few Gironde ministers to office and the speculator Clavière.

The French army had been decimated by the desertion of at least half of the predominantly royalist officer corps. The troops suspected the officers as did the latter the lower ranks. The French armies fled in disarray, with Lafayette drawing back without even having caught a glimpse of the enemy. Outraged at what they considered was desertion at the top, some of the soldiers killed their generals. On May 18, the heads of the army, in violation of the orders they received from the ministries, declared that an offensive was impossible and advised the king to make immediate peace.

The midwife of revolution

Once more war—military defeat this time—proved to be the midwife of revolution. Frederick Engels later commented 'The whole French revolution is dominated by the war of the Coalition, all its pulsations depended upon it'. In war, all that is weak, feeble and rotten is exposed. It pushes to extremes the underlying tensions and class antagonisms in society. The war had broken out against the background of renewed economic crisis and clashes on the issue of food in Paris. It was inflation which, in the spring and summer, together with the war, was to inflame the temper of the masses and give the pendulum of revolution a further swing to the left.

The value of the assignat had dramatically plunged by the early months of 1792. The price of sugar increased from between 22 to 25 sous a pound to between 3 and 3.5 livres. The merchants blamed the rise on the civil war in the West Indies and consequent shortages. The masses believed that the merchants and wholesalers were deliberately hoarding sugar in order to push up the price.

In January 1792, riots broke out in Saint-Antoine, Saint-Marcel and Saint-Denis as well as in the sections of Gravilliers and Beaubourg. In January and February, crowds invaded grocery shops and forced a maximum price of 20 sous a pound of sugar onto the owners. In some instances, these examples of 'popular taxation', the first attempts to limit prices since 1775, were extended to wine, bread, meat and other foodstuffs. In February, a riot broke out in the Faubourg Saint-Marcel, where crowds formed outside a warehouse where 80,000 pounds of sugar had been stockpiled by two speculators. Attempts were made to break into the warehouse, with the women, laundresses amongst them, sounding the tocsin in the church of Saint-Marcel. Petion—the Girondin mayor of Paris—arrived on the scene with armed force, took prisoners and cleared the streets. The two Faubourgs Saint-Marcel and Saint-Antoine where these demonstrations took place played a decisive role in the events later in the year. Without question it was the worsening economic conditions of the masses, allied with the aristocratic conspiracy both internally and externally, which aroused the masses once more to fever pitch.

Girondin propaganda in favour of the war struck a chord amongst the masses. Rouget de Lisle published his song on April 26 in Strasbourg, which became subsequently famous under the title of the *Marseillaise*, the national anthem of the republic. He captured perfectly the mood of France at that stage with a denunciation of traitors, parasites, the 'perfidious' and all the accomplices of 'tyrants'. Revolutionary fervour went hand in hand with love of 'la patrie'—fatherland. The defeats of the French army were attributed to royalist and aristocratic sabotage.

The aristocracy who had remained in France impatiently awaited the arrival of the German army in Paris. Aristocratic insurrections broke out in the south-east and in other areas of the country in expectation that they would link up with the Austrian and German armies. The forces of the revolution in the early months of 1792 in turn organised against the counter-revolution.   In February and March, the Jacobins in Marseilles organised an army which crushed their opponents in Avignon and Arles. From this time, Marseilles was to play a critical role in the revolutionary events of 1792. The Assembly granted an amnesty to all those convicted of acts connected with the revolution. At the same time, the bourgeoisie became alarmed at the direction in which the masses were moving. The masses, not just in Paris but throughout the country, were demanding that everything, particularly the interests of the bourgeoisie, be subordinate to the war.

Agrarian revolt broke out in the countryside around Paris and in the agriculturally rich growing plain of Beauce. Groups of up to eight thousand peasants and rural workers invaded the town markets, imposed their own prices on everything and announced their intention to reduce rents. Some peasants divided up the common lands on their own initiative. In the towns there was intense hostility, particularly on the part of the sans-culottes, to the speculators who tried to profit from the war, who were denounced as counter-revolutionaries.

The deteriorating economic situation, caused by the war and the civil war in the West Indies—where a slave revolution had taken place under the impact of the events in France—led to a clamour for price controls and economic regulation in the early part of 1792. The royalist bourgeoisie gathered around the Feuillants was screaming about threats to the constitution and the danger of 'agrarian law'. The Girondins, holding cabinet positions and linked to the bourgeoisie, could not fail to register the terror of the possessing classes at the emergence of the sans-culottes. Trotsky comments in his *History of the Russian Revolution*:

> How striking is the picture—and how vilely it has been slandered! -of the efforts of the plebeian levels to raise themselves up out of the social cellars and catacombs, and stand forth in that forbidden arena where people in wigs and silk breeches are settling the fate of the nation. It seemed as though the very foundation of society, tramped underfoot by the cultured bourgeoisie, was stirring and coming to life. Human heads lifted themselves above the solid mass, horny hands stretched aloft, hoarse but courageous voices shouted. The districts of Paris, bastards of the revolution, began to live a life of their own. They were recognised—it was impossible not to recognise them!—and transformed into sections. But they kept continually breaking the boundaries of legality and receiving a current of fresh blood from below, opening their ranks in spite of the law to those with no rights, the destitute sans-culottes.

The emergence of the sans-culottes as a major force terrified the Girondins and behind them the bourgeoisie. This was, in time, to drive them towards the right and even force them to seek an accommodation with the king. But in the earlier part of 1792 it was the growing danger of counter-revolution, internally and externally, which pre-occupied the Girondins. Lafayette was openly using his position in the army to assemble the forces to organise a march on Paris, to disperse the clubs and terminate the revolution. The king did not support Lafayette but used his breach with the revolutionaries to dismiss the Girondin ministers. Before then, however, the Girondins were compelled to take action against the gathering counter-revolution.

A series of measures, including the arrest and possible deportation of any priest denounced by 20 citizens, was rushed through the Assembly. The king's constitutional guard was also dissolved. At the same time, 20,000 National Guards were ordered to attend the proposed federation ceremony, to celebrate the taking of the Bastille, and they set up camp outside Paris. The king, however, refused to ratify these measures and instead, on 13 June, dismissed Roland and other Girondin ministers. The Feuillants were returned to power and Lafayette sought to use this situation to strike a decisive blow against Paris and the revolution.

However, the masses of Paris were worked up to an insurrectionary mood by the economic and social situation and the open march of the counter-revolution. Alarmed by the dismissal of the Girondin ministers, they used the pretext of the anniversary of the Tennis Court Oath on 20 June to organise a petition signed by the Gobelins section on behalf of the Faubourgs Saint-Marcel and Saint-Antoine. This requested from the Girondin mayor Pétion the right to parade with arms to present a petition to the Assembly and the king. The bourgeois-dominated municipality and department of Paris supported such a request.

After much to-ing and fro-ing, at five in the morning of 20 June, the sans-culottes in the two Faubourgs, with women and children amongst them, marched on the Tuileries. A section of the sans-culottes entered the royal apartments through a side entrance. For once, royalty was confronted with the real forces of the revolution instead of the ministerial shadows in the assemblies. To roars of 'Down with the veto! Call back the patriot ministers. Tremble tyrants! The sans culottes are here!', the armed mass paraded before the king. He was forced to don the Phrygian cap, the red cap of liberty—recently introduced and made popular by the Girondins as the symbol of revolutionary patriotism—and also joined in toasts to the health of the nation.

This movement proved to be a dress rehearsal for August 10—the 'second French revolution'. Counter-revolution, of course, used the 'indignities' allegedly heaped on the head of the royal family to re-inforce its position. The king refused to give up his veto or to recall the Girondins, and he also proceeded to suspend Pétion and Manuel, officials of the Commune. This was followed by Lafayette appearing before the assembly on 28 June, insisting that strong measures should be taken to 'restore order'. He once more failed to get support and returned to the front, from where he urged the king to join him. Louis refused all offers to flee Paris, but instead counted on the arrival of the Prussian invaders to restore his full authority on the bones of the revolution. As Lefebvre points out, 'He also relied on Girondin vacillation'.

The Girondins for their part accused the king in early July of treason and the assembly declared 'the fatherland in danger'. This resulted in the resignation of the Feuillants on 10 July, with the Girondins hoping that the king would recall them. They secretly opened up correspondence with the king, who gave vague promises as to their possible re-admittance into the cabinet. This resulted in a complete metamorphosis on the part of the Girondins, who were transformed from assailants to defenders of the monarchy. As Rudé points out, they were like 'the sorcerer's apprentice of legend . . . (who) were not prepared to face up to the consequences of the storm that they themselves had let loose'. The vacillation of the Gironde was not an accident. Tied to the bourgeoisie, they were terrified of relying on an insurrection of the sans-culottes which, while it could remove the king, could also make encroachments on 'private property'. They hesitated, and into the breach stepped the Jacobins.

Les aristocrates a la lanterne!

The Second Revolution

THE JACOBINS had played no real part in the movement of 20 June. The Girondins were still in the ascendency in the middle of July, at the anniversary of the storming of the Bastille. But by the end of the month a combination of factors had wrought a profound change in the situation. On 28 July the news reached Paris that the Prussian commander-in-chief, the Duke of Brunswick, had published a brutal, threatening manifesto, at the behest of Marie Antoinette. He warned that if the National Guards resisted the advancing Prussian army, they would meet with summary vengeance.

Threatened on all fronts, the Parisian sans-culottes appealed to the provinces. Five hundred men from Marseilles, 'who knew how to die well', marched to Paris. As they marched they sang the famous 'war song', *La Marseillaise*. Marseilles was the first city to declare for the republic. They were joined by contingents from Brest, Arles and other cities. These *fédérés* bolstered the Parisian sans culottes and, in two petitions in July, demanded that the assembly depose the king. As Lefebvre comments, 'In this sense the revolution of August 10 was not Parisian, as that of July 14 had been, but national'. They set up a central committee with a secret 'directory' which involved some of the leaders of the Parisian sans-culottes.

By the end of July, 47 of the capital's 48 sections had also come out for the king's abdication. By this time, the division between passive and active sections had completely broken down. Parisian sans culottes had in effect penetrated and taken over the sections. It was the section Théâtre Francais which first gave all its members the right to vote. Jacobins and sans-culottes combined together to push aside the 'moderates' and on 30 July, passive citizens were admitted to the National Guard. An executive council, representing the 47 sections, prepared for insurrection. Yet Robespierre was against an armed insurrection, preferring instead replacement of the Assembly by a new Convention elected by manhood suffrage. But the threat of Brunswick and Lafayette, and attempts to mobilise the counter-revolution within the capital itself, forced the Jacobins under the pressure of the masses to reverse their position to one of favouring armed insurrection—an insurrection that was to be organised by the bodies of the sans-culottes themselves.

The insurrection of 10 August

Insurrection threatened to break out on 26 and 30 July but was postponed through the mediating efforts of Pétion. Faubourg Saint-Antoine gave the assembly until 9 August to 'prove itself'. However, a successful insurrection was not automatically guaranteed in the situation which then obtained in Paris. The monarchy concentrated Swiss guards around the Tuileries. They mobilised hundreds of royalists in the capital. They believed they could rely on the National Guard through its commander, Mandat. Louis felt confident that by relying on these forces together with the Prussian troops, he would ensure that the sans-culottes would be crushed. The insurrection on 10 August was a defensive reaction against a renewed offensive of the counter-revolution. It was a decisive situation for the revolution; either the sans-culottes would crush the counter-revolution and its fountain head the king, or the revolution would be annihilated. On the night of 9-10 August, Faubourg Saint-Antoine invited other sections to send representatives to the Hôtel de Ville. The next day, they constituted themselves as the Paris Commune.

This represented a fundamental departure in the revolution. Up to now, the sections had been largely under the sway of the bourgeoisie. But, as Trotsky points out:

> In the bold outbreak of August 10 1792, the sections gained control of the Commune. From then on the revolutionary Commune opposed the Legislative Assembly, and subsequently the Convention, which failed to keep up with the problems and progress of the revolution—registering its events, but not performing them—because it did not possess the energy, audacity and unanimity of that new class which had raised itself up from the depths of the Parisian districts and found support in the most backward villages. As the sections gained control of the Commune, so the Commune, by way of a new insurrection, gained control of the Convention. Each of the stages was characterised by a sharply marked double sovereignty, each wing of which was trying to establish a single and strong government—the right by a defensive struggle, the left by an offensive.

The commander of the National Guard was summoned to the Hôtel de Ville, arrested and executed. The orders that he had given were cancelled, which resulted in the defection or disappearance of the National Guard around the Tuileries. The Girondins then persuaded the monarch to seek refuge in the assembly, believing that this would head off an armed conflict and leave control in the hands of the deputies.

It is absolutely false to present 10 August, as bourgeois historians invariably do, as the armed manifestation of a minority in Paris. On the contrary, it was the culmination of a movement of the masses of Paris clamouring for the dethronement of the king and the setting-up of a republic. A series of what could be called exploratory manoeuvres had taken place in the proletarian areas of Paris.

On the night of 26 and 27 July, there had been a general call to arms led by the Montreuil section of the Faubourg Saint-Antoine, with workers sounding the tocsin at the church of Sainte-Marguerite. The commander of the Saint-Antoine National Guard was aroused from his bed and the workshops remained closed the next day. On 6 August, a mass meeting of Parisians and Fédérés took place on the Champ de Mars with the crowd roaring for the abdication of the king. This mobilisation had prepared a force of 20,000 men which marched on the Tuileries on 10 August. With the defection of the 2000 National Guardsmen, they were met with just 900 Swiss, and just 2-300 Knights of St Louis!

The republicans, with the Marseilles detachments in the front, advanced to fraternise with the Swiss, but were met with a hail of bullets. This recalled the treachery at the Bastille and a serious attack then began. However, the king ordered a ceasefire; this did not save the Swiss who suffered 600 casualties. Ninety Fédérés and also 300 sectionnaires were killed and wounded. Three women were also killed on the side of the assailants. Lefebvre comments: 'July 14 (1789) had saved the Constituent Assembly. August 10 passed sentence on the Legislative Assembly.' The sans-culottes had decided to dissolve the assembly with power vested in their own hands. Yet the leaders of the new Commune were unknown, particularly in the provinces where the Girondins still had considerable support.

Therefore, the Assembly was maintained but a sea-change had taken place in the relationship between the Paris Commune and the assembly. The old Commune had been predominantly middle class, but the new one contained twice as many artisans as lawyers. Moreover, as one commentator put it, the Commune was little more than 'a sort of federal parliament in a federal republic of 48 states'.

The sections came more and more to represent the masses with the admittance of 'passives' to their meetings.

Justices of the Peace and police officers were dismissed and the sections appointed their own organs of justice, with committees appointed to hunt down counter-revolutionaries. At the same time, half the members, the openly royalist bourgeois wing, had fled the assembly on the night of 10 August, and only 284 deputies had remained. This increased the power of the Girondins, who took over all the ministries, with the exception of the Justice Ministry controlled by Danton.

The Assembly also agreed to the election of a National Convention, Robespierre's idea, on the basis of universal suffrage. The king was not immediately dethroned but merely suspended and imprisoned in the Temple. A series of punitive measures were then enacted against feudal counter-revolutionaries. Emigré property had been put under state control in April, but now, with the removal of the king's veto, steps were taken for its sale. This in turn favoured the bourgeoisie, but a section of the peasantry also benefitted. Nevertheless, these measures had not reconciled the revolutionary Paris Commune to the Girondins. The Commune was demanding immediate action for the dethronement and punishment of the king by a special tribunal.

A period of 'competing authorities' developed in Paris and throughout the country. The Assembly sent 'representatives', who were also attached to the army, on missions into the provinces. Danton, who dominated the executive council of the Assembly, sent out commissioners, whereas the Girondin minister, Roland, also had his own agents. At the same time, the Commune appointed its own commissioners who took revolutionary measures, arresting suspects, purging local authorities and ordering arrests.

The Girondins viewed with growing hatred the Commune which 'disorganises everything, is always in the way . . . wants to overturn everything'. The truncated National Assembly with its Girondin majority vied for power with the revolutionary Commune. The left-wing Jacobins, led by Robespierre, leaned on the Commune against the Gironde. Both took punitive measures against internal counter-revolution. These were relatively mild, until the Prussian army crossed the French frontier on 16 August.

Very rapidly, Longwy fell, and by the end of August the Prussians were at Verdun, the last fortress and a bare 200 miles before Paris. The Paris masses prepared to defend the capital, with household searches for arms and the rounding up of suspects throughout the city. The alarm gun was sounded on 2 September, and all citizens were called to the sections. In addition to this, the walls of

Paris were plastered with recruitment posters which urged: 'To arms, citizens, the enemy is at our gate'. Danton, magnificently rising to the occasion, inspired the sans-culottes with his famous call: 'De l'audace, encore de l'audace, toujours de l'audace, et la France est sauvée!' (Audacity, again audacity, always audacity and France is saved). An army of 20,000 sans-culottes marched from Paris to defend the revolution. It was in this situation that the first manifestation of the terror, the 'September massacres' took place.

The massacres

There had been a number of earlier occasions when a 'great fear' had swept through France. During the revolution they were invariably connected in the minds of the masses with counter-revolutionary intrigues by the aristocracy. Fearing a common uprising of the criminal and royalist prisoners and the expected arrival of the Prussian army, some of the sans-culottes took matters into their own hands. Summary executions of suspects took place, beginning on the afternoon of 2 September, and continued over a four day period. Between 1100 and 1400 prisoners were executed, including an estimated 223 priests and an unknown number of aristocrats.

Against this background, Robespierre, on the very day that the massacres began, had condemned Brissot and another Girondin minister Carra as 'Servants of the enemy'. Carra had put forward the idea of setting up Brunswick or the Duke of York as king of France. A thorough search was made of Brissot's residence, and he was only prevented from being arrested by the intervention of Danton.

The September massacres have been inevitably portrayed as the 'senseless outrages of the mob'. Yet, as Lefebvre has pointed out, it was precisely 'The collective mentality' which then existed in France which is the 'explanation for the killing'.

The terror merely accentuated what was already taking place throughout France in the period following 10 August. Stern measures to suppress counter-revolution were undertaken. Repressive measures had been taken against refractory priests, and the remaining monasteries closed. At the same time, divorce was authorised by the assembly. Greater and greater control was exercised over the church, and the rupture between the republican and constitutional clergy was now only a matter of time.

At the same time, the first right-wing insurrection in the Vendée began on 21 August. Brittany was in revolt, and it was the royalists who had organised the surrender of Verdun to the Prussians. The September massacres were, in the eyes of the masses, a necessary 'war to the death' against the counter-revolution. The counter-revolution was even encouraging resistance to enlistment and was praying for deliverance by the Prussians. Savage as it was, the September terror was an inevitable outcome of civil war and, moreover, was mild compared to the treatment which the Parisian masses would have received at the hands of a victorious Prussian army and restored nobility.

The crisis demanded firm measures. Ruthless terror to eliminate the danger of counter-revolution must go hand in hand, reasoned the sans culottes, with the requisitioning of food and other resources, the setting of fixed prices etc, in order to provision the armies. The Commune even attempted a general mobilisation, an anticipation of the later *levée en masse* (mass conscription) which would develop in Year Two of the revolution. The September terror, echoed to some extent in the provinces, at least checked the internal counter-revolution. The French army also halted the Prussians on 20 September.

However, the temporary breathing space did nothing to reconcile the Girondins with the sans-culottes supported by the Jacobins. The bourgeoisie, taken aback at the September terror and at the first beginnings of 'the controlled economy', rallied to the Girondins. They in turn denounced the 'social peril' allegedly emanating from the sans-culottes. On 13 September, Roland denounced the Commune's commissioners and attacked its Vigilance Committee. Temporarily taken aback, the Commune submitted, suspended its Committee and apologised to the Assembly. Nevertheless, it merely replaced it with a new Committee. The Jacobin leadership, who in any case had always adopted a rather ambivalent position towards the actions of the sans-culottes, did not seriously object to the attack on the Commune.

The Convention

These clashes were a precursor to the deadly drama which was to unfold in the newly elected Convention, which first met on 20 September. Out of its 750 members, only 96 were former constituents, while only 190 others had sat in the Legislative Assembly.

From the beginning, the Convention was divided into three main groups: the independent deputies, who, in the great majority, were known as the Plain, and were sometimes described in the semi-insulting term the Marsh. Other parties would acquire prominence and control of the Convention only on the basis of the acquiescence or support of the Plain. The biggest organised group was the Gironde, who sat on the right in the Convention. On the left sat the Jacobins, who were now known as the Mountain, because of the upper tier of seats they occupied in the chamber. They were led by Robespierre and Marat and, at certain times, by Danton. It is from these, partially accidental, seating arrangements that we have acquired the terms of 'right' and 'left' wings.

The differences which ensued between the Gironde and the Mountain in the Convention have been graphically described by the Jacobin deputy Levasseur who participated in the Convention. He comments:

> The only force which existed in France during the interregnum which began on 10 August was the popular élan ... The only means of salvation still remaining was, therefore, to make use of the resources offered and to direct against our enemies the brutal force which it aroused ... The decrees which it [the Legislative Assembly] issued had not the slightest authority. The ministry, product of an impotent assembly, was not itself a real power ... The government therefore passed into the hands of those who knew how to separate themselves from it, that is, to the popular societies in the municipalities. But these improvised centres of government, products of anarchy itself and having no basis in law or in the Constitution, were simply the leaders of the people, powerful as long as they restricted themselves to directing the line of march of the people and giving effect to its wishes; they would not have been able to enforce obedience had they come into conflict with the people.

In relation to the split between the Gironde and the Jacobins, he says:

> It is the Gironde which has separated itself from us. It is Buzot who left the place he had occupied in the Constituent Assembly; it is Vergniaud who abandoned the seat he had recently occupied in the Legislative Assembly ... we were far from seeking divisions ... Pétion [Girondin former mayor of Paris] was nominated president [of the Convention] almost unanimously; the other members of the committee [the Convention Committee, reelected fortnightly] were chosen from amongst the most influential members of the previous Assembly ... Thus when we met the new deputies ... who formed the great majority in the Mountain, they did not even know that there were two camps and that the republicans were not all inspired by the same sentiments and the same aspirations ... The only party which came to the Convention with a complete system and a previously worked out plan took their place in the seats on the right (the

Girondins). By swarming on to the seats opposite ours they declared war on us before they even knew us.

Thus it was the Gironde which went on the offensive against the Jacobins. The Jacobins were prepared to support the Girondin Pétion for the president of the Assembly, whereas the Girondins were the first to separate themselves from the Montagnards (deputies of the Mountain). It was the Girondins who left their former seats on the left and rushed en masse to the righthand side, thus indicating their changed political position. It was they who declared war on the newly arrived republicans who surged to the left, the traditional side of 'patriotism'.

The Jacobins were strong in Paris—23 of the 24 deputies from the capital were Jacobins—but weak in the provinces. The Gironde were weak in Paris where they had used up a lot of their capital because of their vacillations over the August revolution and their attacks on the Commune. Thus the Jacobins were champions of Paris and centralisation—'the republic one and indivisible'—whereas the Gironde promoted the 'federalist' claims of the provinces. Levasseur observed 'The majority of the party of the Gironde were by no means traitors but some were concealed in its ranks. No, it did not desire the ruin of the republic, but its theories led in that direction'. Marx further makes the point: 'The few royalists in the Convention therefore joined forces with them'. Their strength came from the bourgeoisie who had remained monarchist, from the rebellious clergy, and from the partisans of the old regime. All of these forces used the Girondins as a camouflage for their real intentions. A reactionary wrote at the time: 'The two main factions tearing us apart are abominable. Brissot, Pétion and Guadet (Girondins) are as much to be feared as Marat, Danton or Robespierre'. If the Girondins had triumphed with the support of such allies, this would have been a mere episode on the road to reaction. If Kerensky had been victorious in Russia against the Bolsheviks in derailing the revolution, he would soon have been replaced by an open representative of reaction.

Although the majority of the bourgeoisie supported the Gironde, their long term interests were historically expressed by the Jacobins. While they did not enthusiastically support the 'directed economy' and were firm upholders of 'private property', nevertheless they were prepared to echo some of the demands of the masses as a means of defeating reaction and ensuring the safety of the republic. Lefebvre sums up the class forces which lined up behind the Gironde and the Mountain thus:

> Virtually the entire bourgeoisie lined up behind the Girondins, whose name it used as a shield in the Convention and even more

in the provinces, with its royalist tendencies. The Montagnards were elected from Paris and naturally favoured the throng of sans-culottes sectionnaires. The Mountain controlled the Jacobin Club, where it carried on discussions with the sans-culottes, and pleaded their cause.

Yet, in the first period of the Convention the Girondins maintained their popularity as masters of that body. Suspects were freed and many deported priests and emigrés were allowed to return. Controls over the grain trade were abandoned, but the masses still attempted to fix prices which resulted in violence in some areas in December. Under the pressure of Dumouriez, army private contractors linked to him were allowed to make immense profits from the war. The Girondin minister Roland denounced the Commune for keeping down the price of bread, and the peasants were also alienated by the decision to postpone the sale of emigrés' lands.

It was not the Jacobin ministers in the main who opposed these decisions, but the Commune and the sans-culottes. Nevertheless, the Gironde took the offensive against the Jacobin leaders with attacks against Marat and Robespierre as aspiring dictators. On their shoulders was placed the responsibility for the 'September massacres' and an alleged plot to establish a 'revolutionary dictatorship'. Nevertheless, the Plain refused to arraign either Robespierre or Marat, fearing that such a step would undermine the victory gained on 10 August, open the door to the royalists, and thus threaten their gains.

Execute the King!

The Girondins' offensive having been checked, their power waned and they further compromised themselves in the debate over the fate of the king. Robespierre demanded on behalf of the Convention, of the sans culottes and the mass of the French nation that the traitor king be brought before the Convention and sentenced to death. A secret chest of his correspondence had been unearthed after the seizure of the Tuileries which revealed that he was up to his neck in a conspiracy with reaction, including foreign powers, to overthrow the republic by force of arms.

Yet the Girondins temporised, with some of the deputies wanting the king's life to be spared. Their prevarication and obstructionism took the form of arguing that the execution of the king would arouse the ire of feudal Europe who, together with England, would once more endanger the republic. Was it not the Girondins who had argued in November for a revolutionary war to the finish to crush European reaction? The vote on the king's fate took place on 14 January, 1793. The vote against the king was unanimous but when it came to the verdict, out of 721 deputies, 380 voted for the death penalty and 310 were against. The Girondins had split, with some voting for the death of the king and some voting for a reprieve.

On the morning of 21 January, with the entire National Guard lining the route to the scaffold, King Louis XVI was executed. The trial and execution of Louis in France was no more an act of personal spite than the beheading of Charles I by Cromwell and his supporters had been 144 years earlier, on 30 January 1649. It was perceived as necessary in order to safeguard the revolution and to ensure that only a complete carrying through of the revolution offered salvation to the French people.

The Girondins were undoubtedly compromised by their stand on the trial and execution of the king. Yet, as the war party, so long as the republican armies triumphed, they remained supreme in the Convention. The victory of the Republican armies at Valmy in September 1792 was followed by that at Jemappes in November and a wave of enthusiasm swept over France. At the same time, the foreign republican emigrés in France and some of the inhabitants in neighbouring states were agitating for annexation by France. The populations of Nice, Savoy and the Rhineland made such a request. Reacting to this, the Convention offered 'Fraternity and assistance' to all peoples who wished to regain their liberty. In the words of Lefebvre, 'Revolution in France donned warriors garb and challenged the world'. Danton declared 'It is our duty to give freedom to other peoples . . . I declare that we also have the right to tell them 'You will have no more kings".'

The battle cry 'War to the palaces, peace to the cottages' rang from one end of France to another. The Convention had annexed Savoy in November. But the early victories were not maintained. In March, Dumouriez was defeated. He had sent a threatening letter to the Convention which he followed up with an attempt to imitate Lafayette by organising a coup and a march on Paris. Once more however, an aspiring military dictator was deserted by his own army and on 5 April, he crossed over the frontier and deserted to the enemy. Danton, who had attempted to dissuade the general from this course but had been repudiated, was subsequently attacked by the Girondins. He had attempted to play a conciliatory role between the Mountain and the Girondins, but was now driven into the camp of the irreconcilable Jacobins.

The Committee of Public Safety

Under the pressure of the crisis, the Convention passed a series of emergency decrees including the creation of a revolutionary tribunal, a Committee of Public Safety and revolutionary committees in the sections or communes. Thus the 'infamous' Committee of Public Safety, the instrument of 'Jacobin terror', was in fact a creation of the 'moderate' Gironde. At the same time, special agents with the authority of the Convention were dispatched to the provinces as 'representatives on mission'. But the economic and social situation worked to the detriment of the Girondins and to the benefit of the Mountain.

Food prices, after slowing down in the summer and autumn of 1792, shot upwards in the early months of 1793. Sugar more than doubled in price, with big increases in the price of coffee, soap, tallow candles, etc. This resulted in a popular outburst, far more extensive and insistent than the sugar riots of the previous year. Commenting on this, Rudé states:

> ... in this movement, all, or nearly all the Parisian Sections were involved and which, perhaps more clearly than any other incident in the revolution, marked the basic conflict of interests between the *menu peuple* [the common people] and the possessing classes, including the extreme democrats that spoke or applauded at the Jacobin Club, or sat with the Mountain on the upper benches of the National Convention.

Indeed, Saint-Just, along with Girondin spokesmen, had opposed the imposition of price controls on corn. He was denounced in a sans culottes petition as an example of 'fine speakers who eat well every day ... amongst these is the citizen Saint-Just'. The Convention had been petitioned by two deputations of women on 23 February. One of these deputations was made up largely of laundresses who complained about the price of soap. They reminded the deputies that a bill was before the Convention to raise 300,000 recruits for the army which would need the support of the sans-culottes! The Convention spokesmen assured the women that 'an appropriate committee' had the matter in hand. The women withdrew, complaining: 'They adjourn us till Tuesday, but we adjourn ourselves till Monday. When our children ask us for milk we don't put them off until the day after tomorrow'.

Losing patience, on 25 February the masses invaded grocers' and chandlers' shops, forcibly reducing prices. Starting in the Gravilliers section, where Jacques Roux the 'red' priest held sway, the movement spread to the whole of the city. Moreover, the prices which were fixed were roughly the same in all districts, which implied a concerted plan of action probably organised by the supporters of Roux. It was the big merchants and wholesalers who were in the main the objects of mass action. And while the Convention did not respond to the demands of the rioters, the Paris Commune, by subsidising bakers, on 4 March fixed the price of bread at twelve sous for a four pound loaf. The Convention itself was forced to follow suit two months later in also controlling the price of bread and flour throughout the country. This was an anticipation of the famous *maximum général* which was imposed after the purging of the Convention of the Girondins later in the year. In April however, a temporary bread shortage developed and bakers' shops were once more pillaged by angry women. On 2 May, 10,000 unarmed citizens from Saint-Antoine marched before the Convention demanding that prices be controlled, and women from Versailles rioted in the Convention itself, refusing to leave the building. The Jacobins, amongst them Marat, had earlier joined with the Girondins in denouncing the movement to control prices. But now the conflict between the Gironde and the Jacobins had been heightened by the reversals of the French armies and a new outbreak of civil war, particularly in the Vendée. The peasants of this area rose en masse between 10 and 15 March. The nobles assumed the leadership, and several towns and districts were overrun, with both bourgeois and sans culottes being tortured and massacred.

These 'patriots' immediately appealed to the English for assistance to overthrow the revolution. Using favourable terrain for defence and surprise attacks, the Vendéans were able for a time to defeat the 'blues', the National Guard, which was sent against them. But being a largely peasant army, after having won a battle they then retreated to their scattered farms. Their armies were halted on 29 June before Nantes. But the Vendée was to become a running sore and the scene of terrible bloodshed on both sides in the course of the civil war.

The uprising in the Vendée had clear counter-revolutionary aims. Its leading council annulled the sale of church lands in the area it controlled and even decreed that the question of tithes would only be settled after the restoration of the monarchy. Modern bourgeois historians, particularly those on the right like Pierre Chaunu, have retrospectively accused the republican armies of 'genocide' in the Vendée. It is true that the civil war was fought out with great ferocity. The murder of prisoners, collective reprisals, pillage and torture became commonplace. Yet the first to be massacred in the first days of the insurrection were over 500 republicans executed in the small town of Machecoul.

The atmosphere of civil war, the treachery of Dumouriez in

April, combined with the routing of the French armies in the
Rhineland, produced a new 'great fear' which swept over France.
The Girondins, who had been closely associated with Dumouriez,
working on the principle that the best means of defence is attack,
sought to implicate Danton in his betrayal. This in turn forced
Danton into the arms of the Jacobins. Moreover, the Convention,
besieged on the internal and external front, introduced a number
of draconian measures aimed against the counter-revolution. The
death penalty was prescribed for all rebels captured under arms.
Departments were given the authority to deport any clergymen.
Emigres who returned to France were to be executed. Any property inherited by emigrés during the ensuing 50 years was to be
confiscated by the state. The Committee of Public Safety was set
up in April to supervise the executive.

At the same time the Convention, mindful of the betrayal of
Dumouriez, voted to send deputies armed with very wide powers
who were to act as 'political commissars' to each army in the field.
In April and May, the whole of France seemed to be consumed by
upheavals and disturbances. Peasants rose, not just in the Vendée,
but also in Brittany, partly in defence of their clergy and in opposition to forced recruitment into the army.

The divisions between Girondins and Jacobins in Paris were mir-
rored in all the main cities of France. Lyons, Marseilles, Bordeaux
and Nantes were convulsed by clashes between the Girondins and
the Jacobins. In some towns, the Jacobins were victorious, but in
others such as Lyons, Marseilles, Bordeaux and Caen, an anti-
Montagnard coalition held power at the end of May.

In Paris, it was not the Jacobins, but the *enragés* (literally called
'madmen' by their opponents) led by Jean Varlet and Jacques Roux
who initially led the masses in opposition to the Girondin Convention. Varlet, a young radical, made speeches near the Tuileries
to vast crowds of supporters. The *enragés* led by Roux, Varlet
and Leclerc openly campaigned for a ceiling on the prices of all
consumer goods. Varlet demanded the death penalty for hoarders
and speculators and the impeachment of Girondin ministers.

They were attempting to push the Paris Commune into another
journée—a day of revolutionary struggle—an insurrection to overthrow the Girondins in the Convention. Their attempt to do this on
10 March, however, came to nothing. The Jacobins refused to support this movement, considering it premature. They were prepared
to use the popular movement against the Girondins, but its leadership had to be firmly in their hands and not under the control of the
sans culottes' leaders, who had attained recent popularity amongst
the Parisian masses. These included not just Roux, Leclerc and

Varlet but Hébert, the editor of *Le Père Duchesne*, who had gained support both in the Cordeliers and in the Paris Commune.

While the Jacobins wanted the Girondins purged, they feared that too drastic a purge would leave a rump which would then be at the mercy of the sans-culottes. Moreover, they feared that this could lead to a new version of the September massacres and thereby the isolation of Paris. However, it was the offensive of the Girondins against the Jacobins which forced them to ratify an insurrection. Levasseur comments 'It is they (the Girondins) who demanded bills of indictment against their colleagues: It is they who, in handing over Marat to the revolutionary tribunal, violated the immunity of the elected representatives of the people'.

The Girondins had convinced the Convention to send Marat before the revolutionary tribunal. He was promptly acquitted but this 'violation' of the rights of 'elected representatives' set a precedent and was subsequently to be turned against its authors. Moreover, the Girondins sought to back up their successes in the provinces with an offensive in the Paris sections. The battle ostensibly revolved around the method of recruitment to the revolutionary army.

The Commune had adopted a method of recruitment the purpose of which was to excuse 'artisans' and in their place to conscript 'office workers' (the 'golden knee breeches'). Battle royal ensued in the sections between the Girondins and their supporters on the one side, and the Jacobins and the sans-culottes on the other. The Jacobins had jettisoned any previous reservations they may have had concerning an alliance with the sans-culottes. On 5 April, Robespierre's brother Augustin publicly invited the sections to present themselves at the Convention 'to put the unfaithful deputies under arrest'. In late April, Robespierre himself embraced the ideas of the sections and the Cordeliers, in supporting the 'controlled economy'.

In proposing a new Declaration of the Rights of Man, he suggested that property be defined as 'the portion of goods guaranteed by law', but limited its extent by stipulating that it could not prejudice 'the security, the liberty, the existence, or the property of our fellow man'. From a capitalist point of view, this is a complete contradiction. A precondition for the development of capitalism is the alienation of the working class from all 'property', that is, means of production. But nevertheless, it indicated that Robespierre was drawing closer to the sans-culottes.

A bitter class war unfolded in the sections throughout the month of May. Montagnard spokesmen called upon 'locksmiths, carpenters, quarrymen, masons, cabinet makers, in a word, all of you artisans and sans-culottes, working men' to attend the section meetings. Hébert denounced the intervention of the Girondins: 'These villains have had the audacity to seize the registers, to appoint themselves presidents and secretaries. Several revolutionary committees have been dismissed by these brigands and in a word the counter-revolution has triumphed in several sections'. Girondin spokesmen on the other hand openly appealed to the 'haves' against the 'have nots'.   However, at the end of the battle, the sans-culottes and *enragés*, sometimes wielding chairs and other crude weapons, had won control over most of the sections. During this battle, the Girondins launched an offensive against the Paris Commune. They proposed to replace it by the presidents of the sections, but the Assembly decided on the less drastic course of a committee of twelve to investigate the behaviour of the Commune. Made up of Girondins, they sought to strike a blow against the sans-culottes and the Mountain by arresting Varlet, Hébert, the deputy public prosecutor of the Commune and two others. It was clear that the Girondins were preparing to strike a blow at the sans-culottes and the Jacobins. Faced with a life or death battle, with a stark choice facing them, the Jacobins threw in their lot with the sans-culottes, who were themselves preparing for an insurrection.

On 8 May, Robespierre addressed the Parisian masses:

> The armies of the Vendée, the armies of Brittany and of Koblenz are marching against Paris. Parisians! The feudal masters are arming themselves because you are the vanguard of humanity. All the great powers of Europe are equipping themselves against you, and all the base and depraved persons in France support them . . . Parisians! Let us hasten to meet the bandits of the Vendée! Do you know why the Vendée is becoming a danger to us? The Vendée is a danger because great precautions have been taken to disarm a section of the population. But we shall create new republican legions, and we shall not hand over our wives and children to the daggers of the counter-revolution. I asked for money this morning in the Convention for the sans-culottes, for we must deliberate in the sections, and the working man cannot deliberate and work at home at the same time. But he must receive pay for his task of guarding the City. I have asked millions for the sans-culottes of Paris . . . I have asked that people cease calumniating the people of Paris in the Convention and that the newspaper writers who desire to contaminate public opinion have their mouths stopped for them.
>
> I demanded this morning in the Convention, and I demand it here again—and neither in the Convention nor here do I hear any contrary voices—that an army be held in readiness in Paris, an army, not like that of Dumouriez, but an army consisting of sans-culottes and working men. And this army must investigate Paris, must keep the moderates in check, must occupy all posts and inspire all enemies

with terror. We have an immense people of strong sans-culottes at our disposal, who cannot be permitted to drop their work. Let the rich pay!

We have a Convention; perhaps not all its members are poor and resolute, but the corrupt section will for all that not be able to prevent us from fighting. Do you believe that the Mountain has not enough forces to defeat the adherents of Dumouriez, Orléans and Cobourg combined? Parisians, the fate of all France, of all Europe, and all humanity is in your hands. The Mountain needs the People. The People need the Mountain. And I brand the reports that the provinces are turning their arms against the Jacobins as fabrications on the part of our enemies. In conclusion, I demand what I demanded in the Convention this morning, namely, that the Parisians shall be the revolutionary nucleus of the army, strong enough to drag the sans-culottes with them, that an army should remain in Paris in order to keep our enemies in check, that all enemies who are caught shall be placed under arrest, and that money must be confiscated from the rich in order to enable the poor to continue the struggle.

Some of the sections demanded the removal of 22 of the most well known Gironde deputies, which would have purged the Convention and ensured the Jacobins a working majority in it. By mid-April, 35 of the 48 sections had given their support to a rising. The Paris Commune endorsed this, and invited the sections to an assembly out of which a central revolutionary committee was organised. The majority of the executive committee of this body was composed of sans-culottes, with Varlet as part of the leadership. At the same time Hanriot, a former customs officer, was given command of the National Guard. Alongside of this, a 20,000 revolutionary militia of sans-culottes, paid at the rate of 40 sous per day, was organised.

After a false start on 31 May, battalions of the National Guard, supported by an army of sans-culottes, surrounded the Tuileries. Twenty-nine deputies and two ministers, all of them Girondins, were placed under house arrest. However, no action was immediately taken on the social programme of the *enragés*. The Mountain, which had emerged victorious from this battle, pushed aside the insurrectionary committee and replaced it with its own Committee of Public Safety for the department of Paris.

The 1793 Constitution

For the time being, the sans-culottes, the organisers and the force which evicted the Girondins from the Convention, were left empty handed. Yet the Jacobins speedily pushed through the Convention and the primary assemblies the famous Constitution of June 1793. For the first time in history a system of government, which was both republican and democratic, based on the right to vote for all male citizens, was introduced. At the same time, a considerable measure of control was exercised by the population, in theory at least, over the representatives. However, Roux, as a member of a Paris Commune delegation which was congratulating the Convention on this constitution, pointed to its limitations in relation to the poor. This enraged the deputies of the Mountain. Yet Roux returned to the attack later in the month:

> Have you outlawed speculation? No. Have you decreed the death penalty for hoarding? No. Have you defined the limits to the freedom of trade? No. Have you banned the exchange of assignats for specie? No. Deputies of the Mountain, why have you not climbed from the third to the ninth floor of the houses of this revolutionary city? You would have been moved by the tears and sighs of an immense population without food and clothing, brought to such distress and misery by speculation and hoarding, because the laws have been cruel to the poor, because they have been made only by the rich and for the rich ... You must not be afraid of the hatred of the rich—in other words, of the wicked. You must not be afraid to sacrifice political principles to the salvation of the people, which is the supreme law. Admit then that, out of timidity, you accept the discredit of the paper currency, you prepare the way for bankruptcy by tolerating abuses and crimes that would have made despotism blush in the last days of its barbaric power.

The Jacobin and the Bolshevik dictatorships

Notwithstanding Roux's qualifications, the sans-culottes, following the victory of Thermidorean reaction, would later demand the implementation of the 1793 constitution along with bread. The much maligned 'Jacobin dictatorship', like the 'Bolshevik dictatorship' 124 years later, was based upon a constitution which in theory envisaged the greatest democratic republic ever seen up to that point. The fact that it was not implemented was not due to the alleged 'dictatorial' tendencies of Jacobinism, but arose, like the terror itself, from the objective situation of the revolution which was besieged by reaction on all sides. Although different class forces were involved in the Russian revolution, the Bolsheviks faced a similar situation as the Jacobins in France. The Soviet constitution which followed the October revolution of 1917, with power vested in the hands of soviets, with the right of re-call over all soviet deputies etc, was the most democratic in history. Yet, it could not be fully implemented because of a devastating civil war and the intervention of the 21 armies of imperialism. Emergency powers which effectively emasculated the soviets were vested in the hands of the Bolsheviks, the most democratic and revolutionary party in history.

The Bolshevik leadership, like the Jacobins before them, hoped that with the defeat of the counter-revolution, the soviets would be restored and freedom given to all of those who accepted the basis of the revolution. In the bourgeois revolutions, not only in France, but also in the English revolution of the seventeenth century, force was required to hold down the feudal counter-revolution. But the British bourgeoisie of the twentieth century do not need to employ force against advocates of a return to feudalism, to 'merrie England' (which was not so merry for the mass of the population). The advantages of bourgeois society over feudalism are no longer in dispute. However, things stood rather differently in the seventeenth century. Then, Cromwell was compelled to resort to the sword to suppress the advocates of feudalism and also to cut off the head of a king. The 1793 French constitution was prefaced by a new declaration of rights amplifying the 1789 version, with provisions for religious liberty, economic freedom and the institution of 'political democracy'. Its main provisions allowed for a legislative body, elected by direct, universal male suffrage with single member districts. The executive council was to be chosen by the legislative body and provisions were allowed for the holding of referendums. The constitution itself would be ratified by the people. It also proclaimed that the aim of society was 'the general welfare', stipulating poor relief, a 'sacred obligation', as a right of the poor.

While introducing the Constitution, the Convention also ratified the sale of the property of emigrés to the peasants, in small parcels to be paid for over ten years. This was seen as a means of binding the peasants, particularly the small peasants, to the revolution. This decree proposed the optional division of common lands by head. On 17 July, the Convention also carried through the famous abolition, without compensation, of all that remained of manorial rights. This merely ratified 'juridically' what the peasants had in effect carried through themselves. Yet it completed the task of eliminating feudal rights which had been left unfinished in the wake of the 1789 revolution.

The power of the sans-culottes

THE OPPONENTS of the Jacobins, particularly in the provinces, were not reconciled to the June overturn in Paris. A new civil war broke out. In Brittany, Normandy, Franche-Comté and in the south, the departmental administrations seceded. They had, in effect, been in open revolt since March but now, in Lyons, Marseilles, and Toulon, 'popular' tribunals ordered patriots to be guillotined or hanged. Even in Paris, a number of sections in the centre and the west were controlled by the 'moderates' and behind them stood the royalists. Toulon was preparing to surrender to the English and its re-capture by the republic provoked a civil strife every bit as ferocious, including bloody reprisals, as in the Vendée. As Lefebvre has pointed out: 'In July it had seemed that France was disintegrating'.

On top of this, the economy deteriorated further. The assignat slumped in value between June and August. The problem of food and prices had remained unsolved. The revolution of May and June had done little to remedy this. Price increases outstripped wages and attacks were once more made on the wealthy shopkeepers and wholesalers. A worker declared: 'It is known that this class in general is the only one to have profited from the revolution'. Riots over the price of soap broke out in late June, which led to the outburst of Roux mentioned earlier. The Parisian masses inundated the Convention with demands for the introduction of a maximum, a ceiling on prices, coupled with demands to curb inflation and restrain speculation. The masses indissolubly connected the revolution's mortal combat with its external and internal enemies with a war against the 'selfish rich'. No compromise was possible with the Coalition of European powers, who wanted to restore the old regime. The Austrians in some areas, such as the Nord, which they had re-occupied, restored feudalism.

81

The September insurrection

Voices amongst the sans-culottes demanded the death penalty against hoarders, even the closing of the stock exchange and the suppression of joint stock companies, the quintessence of capitalism itself. In this situation the idea of another march, an 'insurrection', to enforce the demands of the sans-culottes, grew. In July and August the remaining strongholds of bourgeois and conservative elements in the Parisian sections had been purged. Growing discontent culminated in the 'insurrection' of 4-5 September which, after some hesitation, the Paris Commune supported.

It began with the building workers joining with others from the workshops who then converged in a demonstration near the Ministry of War. The Commune's leaders, Hébert and Chaumette, first of all tried to dissuade the demonstrators, but then agreed to a march on the Convention the next morning. Workshops were ordered to close the next day, and masters and journeymen were urged to join the demonstration. The issues of prices and food supplies were played down. Yet the decisions taken in the wake of this demonstration left their mark on the subsequent development of the revolution. On the one side, needy sans-culottes were to be compensated with 40 sous per attendance at the section meetings, while, on Danton's initiative, the number of section meetings were cut down to two a week. This expressed the fear, not just on the part of Danton, but also of the Jacobin leadership as a whole, of their sans-culottes allies.

However, mass pressure for price controls was irresistible. On 29 September the Convention passed the famous *maximum général*. This put a limit on the prices of a large range of essential goods and services, including that of labour. Prices were limited to those which existed in the departments in June 1790 plus one third. At the same time, wages were raised by 50 per cent. A police agent was to report: 'The people have been overjoyed by the news of the decrees passed by the National Convention on price ceilings for food and staples of prime necessity'. By this measure, the Jacobin Convention seemed to cement the alliance between it and the sans-culottes which had effected the June overturn and was the foundation of the revolutionary government in Year Two of the republic. This government lasted from the summer of 1793 to the summer of 1794.

The sans-culottes had made significant advances, with the right to vote and now, it seemed, cheap food and the control of supplies. The Jacobins on their part, by leaning on the sans-culottes, had risen to power and crushed their Gironde opponents. They ruled in the Convention, with the sans-culottes' representatives almost totally excluded, while the latter controlled the Paris Commune, the section assemblies and the clubs, the local revolutionary committees and battalions of the National Guards. However, as Rudé has commented, this alliance was 'riddled with contradictions, the partnership could not last long: these had already become apparent on the morrow of the common victory and will become far sharper in the critical months ahead'. Its bonds already loosened in October 1793, by the summer of 1794 the alliance lay in ruins and brought down both partners in its fall.

A new revolutionary government had begun to take shape in France at the beginning of July. Its core consisted of Couthon, Saint-Just, and those like Barère who had come over from the Plain. Lindet and Robespierre joined them on 27 July. Carnot, Billaud-Varennes and Collot d'Herbois also joined on 6 September. As Lefebvre has pointed out, 'Although they all belonged to the bourgeoisie, it was primarily social leanings that separated Robespierre or Saint-Just, who were partisans of a social democracy, from Carnot or Lindet, who were distinctly conservative'. These men controlled the committee which exercised power in the name of the Convention. Yet it had been barely assembled when it was beset on all sides by new disasters.

On 13 July 1793, Marat was assassinated by Charlotte Corday, a young royalist from Normandy, and three days later the 'moderates' in Lyons beheaded Chalier. Janet, an historian hostile to the Jacobins, was to write a hundred years later: 'Enemy troops invaded French territory from four sides: from the north, the English and Austrians; in Alsatia, the Prussians; in the Dauphiné, proceeding as far as the city of Lyons, the Piedmontese; and in Roussillon, the Spaniards. And all this at a time when civil war raged on four sides: in Normandy, in the Vendée, in Lyons and in Toulon'. Plekhanov comments:

> The government, which had taken up the struggle against these innumberable inner and outer foes, had neither money nor sufficent troops: it could count on nothing but a boundless energy, the active support of the revolutionary elements of the country and the colossal courage to shrink from no measure, however arbitrary, illegal or ruthless, so long as it was necessary for the defence of the country.

Trotsky showed later, that it was not just the young French republic, but the bourgeoisie of the United States during their Civil War who also resorted to 'terroristic' measures to suppress the slave owners, their press and their supporters in the northern states.

In July and August, reaction appeared to have the revolution by the throat. Over a period of three weeks, Mainz capitulated to the Prussians and the Austrians seized the frontier fortress of Condé and invaded northern France. Spanish troops crossed the Pyrenees and advanced on Perpignan and, in Corsica, Paoli led a revolt with British naval support which expelled the French from the whole island. In addition to this, the siege of Dunkirk was opened by the British in August and October, and coalition forces invaded Alsace. At the same time, the royalists had seized some important provincial centres such as Lyons and Marseilles.

On 12 July, the Convention forces besieged Lyons, taking it in August. They followed this up by capturing Marseilles on 25 August, just in time to prevent it from capitulating to the British fleet which was cruising offshore. In Toulon, the counter-revolution handed the town and the arsenal over to the British fleet proclaiming Louis XVII as king. Twenty-six of the republic's 65 ships of the line and 16 of its 61 frigates were handed over to the enemy. This was 'a disaster worse than Trafalgar'. Modern bourgeois historians, eager to criticise the 'bloodthirsty' Robespierre, conveniently pass over the causes of the terror. Robespierre himself declared to the Convention: 'In two years, 100,000 men have been butchered because of treason and weakness. It is weakness for traitors that is destroying us'.

The numbers who went to the guillotine during the Montagnard dictatorship were minimal compared to those who perished on the battlefield. Plekhanov points out:

> After the Montagnards had called to arms the entire French youth, without being able to supply the newly formed armies even partially with arms and food out of the slender means flowing to them from taxation, they resorted to requisitions, confiscations, forced loans, decreed rates of exchange for the assignats—in short and in fine, they forced upon the scared possessing classes money sacrifices, all in the interests of an imperilled country for which the people were sacrificing blood.

The iron determination and energy of the Jacobins bolstered by the sans-culottes was all that stood between the revolution and the triumph of reaction. Twenty years later, a member of the Committee of Public Safety, Jeanbon St André, would declare:

> Do you know what kind of government was victorious? A government of passionate Jacobins in red bonnets, wearing rough woollen cloth, wooden shoes, who lived on simple bread and bad beer and went to sleep on mattresses laid on the floor of the meeting halls, when they were too tired to deliberate further. That is the kind of men who saved France.

Up to August-September 1793, measures against the counter-revolution were relatively mild. Under the pressure of the demonstration of 5 September, however, the Convention made terror 'the order of the day'. Between 6 and 8 September, measures were introduced resulting in the arrest of any enemy nationals and the confiscation of their property. Seals were placed on the houses of bankers and stockbrokers and, on 9 September, the revolutionary army was organised under the command of Ronsin.

On 17 September, the 'Law of Suspects' was agreed to by the Convention. This was followed by the obligatory wearing of the tricolour cockade. Thus, throughout September the Convention steadily moved toward the implementation of the 'controlled economy'. This went hand in hand with the stepping-up of the terror. From October to December, executions were increased with the guillotining of Marie Antoinette on 16 October. She was followed to the scaffold by the 21 Girondins, including their leader Brissot who perished on 31 October.

The Girondin leaders were eliminated either through execution, suicide or mass arrests. At the same time, the Jacobins took steps to distance themselves from the more 'extreme' sans-culottes. Roux and Varlet were arrested and Leclerc disappeared. However, the Jacobin convention enjoyed colossal authority and support from the sans culottes. The *levée en masse* had raised a million men, and on 10 October, on the initiative of Saint-Just, the Convention finally proclaimed that 'the provisional government of France is revolutionary until the peace'.

War to the death against feudal reaction was now decreed by the revolutionary government. When this decree was read out in the Convention, one of the deputies cried out: 'Have you then concluded a treaty with victory?' The answer was: 'No, we have concluded a treaty with death'.

The Committee, however, invested its hopes in the rank and file, predominantly sans-culottes, rather than the officers, many of whom were still suspected of royalist sympathies. The Jacobins were in a similar situation to that which faced the Bolsheviks after they took power. The latter were compelled to rely on former Tsarist generals in the early days of building the Red Army, but checked their actions through widespread democracy amongst the army's ranks and by a system of 'political commissars'. In France, the same functions were undertaken by the representatives of the Committee appointed to each army. Thus the Committee wrote to its representatives with the army of the Rhine on 6 October 1793: 'Watch the generals. Make no allowance for them. When the armies are endangered it is almost always because of their treason'.

THE MASSES ARISE

The economic situation of the masses had improved as a result of the introduction of the *maximum général*. Its introduction had the immediate effect of both guaranteeing the support of the sans-culottes and of arresting inflation.

In the three months that followed the introduction of the maximum, the value of the assignat also improved dramatically. The police reports at the time record the hopes of the masses who connected the cheap and adequate food that they received with early victory for the republic: 'The workers who gather in great numbers at meal times in front of the city hall on the square rejoice at the reduction in staple prices, at the ardour of the youths being conscripted, and especially at the imminent victory of the republic'.

Robespierre's stock had risen with the improvement in the conditions of the masses. The most oppressed layers were enamoured of the Convention as another report indicated 'The market women are in a gay, charming mood; they sing the praises of the Convention'. This was the period when the power of the sans-culottes was at its height. They were dominant throughout the Paris administration. Their militants held sway in the sectional assemblies and committees, in the revolutionary committees, in the general assembly and in the executive of the Commune.

Out of the 454 members of the revolutionary committees holding office in Paris in the course of Year Two, it has been estimated that 9.9 per cent were wage earners, 63.8 per cent were shopkeepers, small workshops masters and independent craftsmen, while only 26.3 per cent were rentiers, manufacturers, civil servants, and members of the 'liberal professions'.

The period after the September 'insurrection' and the implementation of the *maximum général* to the end of 1793 was the period of the greatest power of the sans-culottes. The authority of the Committee of Public Safety remained precarious. It was the sans-culottes who applied revolutionary measures, not just in Paris, but throughout the country. The representatives on mission from the Convention, surrounded on all sides by the hostility of local notables who were often closet Girondins, were forced to purge the local authorities and drew on the energy and revolutionary devotion of the local sans culottes. Thus, an agent of the Minister of the Interior wrote on 24 September 'I think the majority of the municipalities need to be changed so as to exclude big landowners and farmers who keep the other citizens in a state of dependence so that they don't dare to say a word'.

The bourgeoisie were elbowed aside in Nantes and the municipality was made up of many sans-culottes with no wealthy merchants on the council. In some of the country areas, the councils were controlled by day labourers and yeoman farmers. In one area, the members of the municipal council were illiterate, and sometimes the Justices of the Peace could hardly write while others could barely sign their names. Inevitably, the sans-culottes' dictatorship at local and regional level was disorganised and anarchistic, but the Committee in Paris, groping towards the organisation of a government, was forced to base itself on them in the first period. The educated were also the wealthy, with Girondin and royalist sympathies. Nevertheless, the picture which has been presented of the sans-culottes as a disorganised rabble is completely false. Lefebvre comments:

> When the government failed to act, it was the impetus of the Jacobins and deputies on mission that saved the republic in the summer of 1793. They re-established national unity, recruited and supplied the armies and fed the population. Nevertheless, there had been a surfeit of authorities and a lack of co-ordination and discipline. Arrests and taxes were causing anger, the revolutionary armies might be turned against the Convention, and local conflicts threatened to disorganise administration, or at least to reduce the effectiveness of the war effort. The spontaneous popular action had been salutary, but (as Levasseur noted) 'Anarchy' could not continue. The Committee deemed it necessary to organise the regime and to reinforce centralisation.

Robespierre in particular was determined to overcome the administrative anarchy that appeared throughout the country. The sans-culottes in Paris had circumvented the outlawing by the Convention of daily meetings of the sections and formed 'Sectional popular societies' which met on the nights when the sections themselves were not in session. Some of the local committees had raised *armées revolutionnaires*, sometimes from the unemployed, and powerful 'pro-consuls' like Fouché, Tallien and Carrier interpreted and applied the law in their own fashion in the provinces.

The need for a strong hand at the centre convinced the Committee that the power of the Paris government should be strengthened at the expense of local control and improvisation. This in turn required that the constitution of June 1793 should be put aside until such time as the counter-revolution had been defeated. The views of the Committee were summed up in the law of 4 December 1793 which vested full executive power in the Committees of General Security and Public Safety. They derived their authority from the Convention.

Bourgeois historians who accuse Robespierre of all along wishing to exercise a dictatorship, conveniently pass over the fact that the deputies of the Plain accepted these emergency measures as did those of the Mountain. Thus the republican bourgeoisie, who were in a majority in the Convention, were prepared to sanction the most extreme revolutionary measures in order to safeguard the gains of the revolution.

It was the support of the Plain between June 1793 and July 1794 which was one of the factors which sustained Robespierre in power. So long as the counter-revolution remained a threat, they would continue to support Robespierre, no matter how reluctantly or distastefully they looked on the 'terror'. Only when circumstances changed, when it appeared as though counter-revolution had been driven from the soil of France, did their attitude towards the Montagnards in turn undergo a transformation.

The two great committees exercised a division of labour. That of General Security was responsible for the police and internal security, including the revolutionary tribunal, the work of the local vigilante and revolutionary committees. The Committee of Public Safety, on the other hand, had greater powers—to control ministers, appoint generals, conduct foreign policy and to purge and direct local government. As well as overruling local authorities, the Committee replaced local procureurs of departments and communes with its own 'national' agents answerable to it.

At the same time, the independence and powers of the Paris Commune were severely curtailed. It was prohibited from sending commissioners to the provinces, its control over the National Guard was limited and the 'revolutionary' committees of the Sections came under the control of the Committee of General Security. The terror which up to now had been improvised was now directed from the centre. Rudé correctly comments: 'It was the end of anarchy, but it was the beginning of the end of popular initiative as well'. Inevitably, the measures of the centralised, strong government provoked opposition from those who suffered at its hands. But it also came from precisely within the Jacobins' own ranks and in the ranks of their allies in the Cordeliers Club.

Almost as soon as the Montagnards had taken power in June, divisions opened up in the Jacobin Club, with Hébert and his supporters clamouring for violent and extreme measures against reaction and the rich. They were opposed on the right by Danton. Around him gathered the so-called party of 'indulgents'. Their opponents claimed they were indulgent towards the rich and the threat of counter-revolution. Danton had been dismissed from the Committee of Public Safety after its re-organisation on 10 July; he now retired with his wife to a country estate. Where he had acquired the money for this farm was a mystery and has been since then a cause of endless speculation. The Robespierrists and some historians have suggested this came from bribes which he received from rich friends, those 'corrupt' ones who had grown fat on the war.

The main aim of the Dantonists was to break up the 'revolutionary government', to restore the freedom of action of local authorities, to dismantle the machinery of terror and to abandon the controlled economy. Above all, they argued for a negotiated peace, placing their hopes on the detachment of England from the European coalition. On 22 November, Danton declared: 'I asked that the blood of man be spared'. Yet the foreign invaders had not yet been driven from the soil of France. The sans-culottes denounced such proposals as treason.

The opposition of the Hébertists represented, if anything, a greater threat to Robespierre. Danton enjoyed some support in the Convention, but the Left was powerful in the Cordeliers Club, the Paris Commune, the *armées revolutionnaires*, the clubs and Sections etc. The Jacobin leaders had already given notice of their attitude toward the most 'extreme' sans-culottes, with the repression of the *enragés* and the subsequent suicide of their leader Roux. Nevertheless, Hébert, in his journal *Le Père Duchesne*, echoed the demands of the sans-culottes for a more vigorous prosecution of the war and of the scaffold for hoarders and speculators. Hébert, together with Chaumette and Fouché (who was soon to switch sides, ending up as the police chief of Bonaparte), energetically supported the campaign for 'Dechristianisation'. War was declared on the Christian religion in both Paris and the provinces. The sans-culottes carried through the wholesale closure of churches. They defrocked priests and bishops, and enthroned the 'Goddess of Reason' in a special ceremony at the Cathedral of Notre Dame.

Every place of religious worship was closed down by the Commune in November. The Convention had shown its hostility to Christianity with the adoption of a totally new 'republican' calendar on 7 October. Accordingly, the new republican era began with the abolition of the monarchy on 22 September 1792. The year was divided into twelve months with thirty days, with five supplementary 'sans culottides' at the end. The months, at first known merely as 'first', 'second', etc, were given names illustrating the seasons to which they applied: Ventôse, Floréal, Thermidor, etc.

The new calendar was supposed to symbolise the substitution of 'reason' for tradition, the cult of an idealised nature and a breach with christianity. The Christian festivals disappeared overnight, along with Sunday, and the week became a 'decade' of ten days. The rest-day became a 'decadi' and Sunday was a working day.

However, the attempt to abolish the Catholic religion and worship was correctly attacked by Robespierre and the majority in the Convention as a major error. They were prepared to sanction the separation of the Church from state, but, faced on all sides with enemies, they could not afford to drive devout Catholics, in the towns but particularly in the rural areas, into the arms of reaction. Meanwhile, the undermining of the *maximum général*, inevitable on the basis of capitalism, brought the Committee into more and more conflict with the sans-culottes and their Hébertist leaders.

Front cover of Hébert's Pere Duchesne

Germinal

IN THE AUTUMN of 1793, the government was forced to resort to economic regulations, including the effective nationalisation of foreign commerce. It also attempted to conciliate the peasants, the lower middle class, the artisans and shopkeepers by omitting some items from control. Thus as early as October 1793, the Convention decreed that livestock would be exempt, which in effect circumvented price controls on meat. While the sans-culottes and the *armées revolutionnaires* sought to check the hoarding of food, the Committee of Public Safety countered this by forbidding house to house searches in Paris and elsewhere. Through the medium of an army of middle men, a thriving black market developed. A pound of butter sold at twice the control price and eggs at sometimes two and three times the control price.

The sans-culottes bitterly complained but tended to blame the merchants and the shopkeepers rather than the government. They called for sterner action by the government and a harsher implementation of the 'economic terror' against the 'selfish rich'. The government was caught between two fires, the need to conciliate the peasants and producers by amending the regulations and increasing the profits of business, and the demands of the sans-culottes for greater repression. A ferocious struggle unfolded in early 1794 between the three factions: the Robespierrists, the Dantonists or 'indulgents', and the Hébertists. Robespierre at first leaned on the Dantonists, in a joint campaign against 'dechristianisation', in order to crush the Left. However, this emboldened the Right. Through the mouthpiece of Desmoulins' journal *Le Vieux Cordelier*, they campaigned for the lifting of the terror, negotiations with the enemy, and the abandonment of the controlled economy.

Robespierre, who had zig-zagged between both factions, first leaning on one and then the other, now concluded that it was necessary to strike blows against both factions. Robespierre's actions were determined by the stage which the revolution had reached. Engels wrote later:

> As far as the terror is concerned, it was a *war measure* in so far as it had a meaning. Not only did it serve to maintain at the helm the class, or fraction of a class, which alone could secure victory for the revolution, but also assured it freedom of movement, elbow room, the possibility of concentrating its forces at the decisive points—the frontiers.

The attack on the Hébertists

The Robespierrists, the revolutionary petit bourgeois democracy, and the bourgeoisie gathered in the ranks of the Plain, perceived both the Commune and the Dantonists as opponents—the Commune with its frenzied defence of plebeian democracy and decentralisation, and the Dantonist 'indulgents' who wished to conciliate the counter-revolution. The power, or subsequent impotence, of leading figures in the revolution, such as the Girondin leaders, then Danton or later Robespierre himself, lay not primarily in their personal strengths and weaknesses but in the objective reality reflected at each stage in the revolution.

Hundred of books and millions of words have been spent in seeking to explain the confused, passive and puerile attitude of Danton in the last months of his life. However, the same disorientation and passivity beset Robespierre on the eve of his downfall. The explanation for this phenomenon is that they represented certain social formations which, having played a progressive role, then came into conflict with the further progress of the revolution. At a certain stage, they exhausted all political possibilities and could not move decisively forward because of 'over-powering reality'.

Changed conditions in the internal economic situation, international factors and not least the changed outlook of the masses, converted formerly powerful figures such as Danton or Robespierre into helpless figures in the face of hostile historical currents. Of course, this or that mistake could accelerate or decelerate the process as the case might be, but it was the objective situation which determined the fate of personalities and groupings at each stage in the French revolution.

In the period leading up to the elimination of the Hébertists, the discontent of the sans-culottes at the deterioration in their economic situation began to be directed against the government itself.

In late February, a woman worker declared to a group of others:

'If I were not restraining myself I would tell the new regime to go shove it'. Bread became scarce and inedible with the peasants, intimidated by the sections' commissionnaires, bringing in less and less of their produce. Meat was in short supply and the Hébertists, incited the sans-culottes to demand stringent measures, whilst strikes broke out in the arms factories. Under the pressure of massive discontent, Saint-Just obtained a decree confiscating the property of suspects and distributing it amongst the needy. The left in the Cordeliers Club believed that if it only stepped up the pressure, it would triumph once and for all. Ronsin, head of the Paris National Guard, spoke of the need for a new insurrection along the lines of September 1793. All that was intended was probably a demonstration, but the police reported that a section of the sans-culottes were arming themselves for a new *journée*.

To begin with, the Jacobins attempted a reconciliation but were rebuffed by the Cordeliers Club. Therefore, the Committee decided to strike a death blow at the Hébertists. Along with their leader Hébert, Ronsin and Vincent were also arrested, and, for good measure, foreign revolutionaries domiciled in Paris. This was done in order to sustain the fiction that the Hébertists were linked with a 'foreign plot'. Again, it is impossible here not to draw an analogy with the Russian revolution following the victory of reaction and the accusations by Stalin that Trotsky and the Opposition were agents of 'foreign powers'. The Hébertists were executed on 4 Germinal (24 March). Five days before this the 'corrupt' ones—the friends of Danton, Fabre d'Eglantine, Chabot, Basire, Delaunay—had been arrested and charged. The Committee then added Danton, Camille Desmoulins and two others, concluding that, having struck down the left, it was necessary to deal a blow against the right.

At first, Robespierre hesitated to sanction the execution of Danton, 'the long decayed idol'. Under pressure of others on the Committee, however, he accepted and 'took it upon himself to quash the protest in the dismayed and trembling Convention'. Added to the list of Dantonists were some well known speculators and a group of 'foreigners' who were there to justify the 'foreign plot'.

The Dantonists were executed on 5 April 1794, and were followed by a mixed 'batch' among whom were Chaumette from the Commune, Hébert's widow, and Lucille Desmoulins, Camille's wife. Historians have had to agree that the guillotining of Danton, 'though distasteful to former associates in the Convention, caused not a ripple of protest in the Sections nor among the sans-culottes'. They differ, however, as to the reaction amongst the sans-culottes at the execution of Hébert. While the mood may have been one of apathy rather than anger, the majority of the sans-culottes could not fail to be stunned by the execution of the editor of *Le Père Duchesne* and leader of the Commune together with the commander of the revolutionary army, and Vincent. Lefebvre considered that the execution of the Hébertists marked a decisive turning point in the revolution:

> In the history of the revolutionary movement the fall of the Hébertists marked the beginning of the ebb tide. For the first time since 1789, the government had forestalled popular action by doing away with its leaders . . . Next to the *enragés*, *Le Père Duchesne* and the Cordeliers had been the real leaders of the sans culottes.

The government followed up with a ruthless purge of all the former strongholds of the sans-culottes. The *armées revolutionnaires* were disbanded on 7 Germinal, Year 2 (27 March 1794). The Ministry of War was purged, as was the general council of the Commune and the police, which was filled with stooges of the government. This was followed with a decree whereby the Commission on Provisions assumed control of supplying Paris with bread and meat. The Cordeliers Club was reduced to impotency. The Jacobin Club and the Cordeliers became rubber stamps for the government, later recording 100 per cent votes for the government. The popular societies, which had lain outside the formal structures of the Jacobins, were also effectively destroyed.

The threat of reaction

The corresponding disappointment of the masses was recorded by police observers, one of whom reported just after the execution of the Hébertists: 'The people no longer trust anyone'. A week later he continued: 'In the cafés . . . one observes that those who talked a great deal are no longer saying anything'. Another worker was heard to exclaim 'What can we expect . . . when we are betrayed by the people we have most confidence in'. This disappointment was deepened with the further undermining of the concessions which the sans-culottes had enjoyed in the previous period. The agitation in the market over the allocation of eggs and butter continued in March and an unemployed worker was arrested for shouting 'Fine liberty we have! It was made for the rich; the only war being waged was against the poor'.

The Committee amended the maximum in late March. This provided for higher prices and profit margins accompanied inevitably with the growth of speculation. The growing anger of the masses was reflected in a letter sent by the laundresses of the Faubourg Saint-Marcel who denounced General Hanriot, commander-in-chief of the National Guard, as a 'wretched hanger-on of Robespierre'. There was an even greater outburst of anger when the revised maximum was applied to wage rates.

The *maximum général*, introduced in Sèptember 1793, had not only stipulated the reduction in prices, but also limited wages - but by a smaller percentage. These reductions did have an effect in some trades, where workers' resistance was likely to be weak. However in Paris, where the Hébertist Commune was in control and where there was a labour shortage, wages rose between two and three times above their pre-revolutionary level. But in the government-controlled workshops, attempts were made to rigidly apply lower wage rates, buttressed by a severe disciplinary code aimed against 'agitators'. Therefore, when Hébert was out of the way and the Commune reduced to impotence, the government prepared, with fatal consequences, measures to lower wages.

At the same time, they applied the notorious Le Chapelier Law, which effectively outlawed trade unions. When plasterers, bakers, pork butchers and port workers struck for increased wages, the matter was sometimes referred to the police. After a short lull, the movement started up again amongst the arms workers in June. It spread to other branches, but the ring leaders in a number of the workshops were arrested on the spot, while others left their shops in search of better pay and less restricted conditions elsewhere. Barère denounced the workers who struck and instructed the revolutionary tribunal to take action against what he called 'the counter- revolutionaries who have employed criminal methods in the workshops.' A clamour for increased wages developed throughout June and July, with workers in the building trades, potters, etc, pushing for increases. On 7 July, even the Committees' own printing workers struck work, leading to the arrest of three of the leaders. It was against this background that the Paris Commune on 23 July, with immaculate timing, coming as it did around the time of Robespierre's downfall, published new wage rates to operate in the capital. The authorities took absolutely no account of recent increases in either wages or food prices. The great majority of the working population were now faced with substantial reductions, sometimes amounting to one half or more of their existing earnings.

The alienation of the sans-culottes was deepened by these measures. They were to play their part, in the apathy and passivity so evident at the time of Robespierre's overthrow. The Committee believed that it had assured its domination by the double blow against the Hébertists on the left and the 'indulgents' on the right in late March and early April. But it had alienated itself, particularly the Robespierre faction within the Committee, both from the bourgeois National Convention and from the plebeian sans-culottes.

The Committee believed that the elimination of the Dantonists had assured it a safe majority in the Assembly. But the existence of so many 'empty seats' spread a secret terror amongst the Assembly members; nobody felt safe from the guillotine. The Committee had assured its position as a mediator between the Assembly and the sans- culottes. But now, by breaking with the sans-culottes, it freed the Assembly, and to complete its self-destruction, it only had to split internally. More importantly, the power of the Committee of Public Safety was only secure just so long as the revolution was threatened by the royalists internally and while foreign troops still occupied French soil. Once these dangers were lifted, the bourgeoisie's yearning to enjoy the spoils of their victory over feudalism in tranquillity and peace was to topple Robespierre. Personal grievances and personality splits within the Committee, although playing a part in the downfall of Robespierre and his group, were nevertheless subordinate to the decisive changes in the objective situation.

Only with the greatest difficulties and by summoning up the colossal revolutionary energies of the masses did the republican armies vanquish the counter-revolution. As Lefebvre put it: 'The will to conquer was universal. Without exception the Montagnards sacrificed everything to the army'. Through the *levée en masse*, raised and organised by the organisational genius of Carnot, an irresistible force was fashioned which smashed royalist internal revolt and the armies of the Coalition.

The royalist insurrections are defeated

In August 1793, the royalist insurrections were largely reduced but at terrible costs to both sides. Thus, in Lyons, declared a 'freed city' after its liberation by republican forces, ruthless repression, involving the demolition of the houses of the rich, and mass executions took place. By March of 1794, 1667 death sentences had been pronounced by revolutionary committees. At the same time, the first war of the Vendée—the scene of the most vicious massacres on both sides of the whole revolution—was terminated.

In September 1793, the royalist armies—the 'whites'—suffered a setback, but then, joining up with the bands of Jean Chouan, reached Angers in December. Terrible street fighting took place in Le Mans, but the Vendéan forces were annihilated on 23 December. The republican forces then implemented the plan of 'devastation' that had been decreed by the Convention on 1 August. Bourgeois and royalist historians have described the repression effected by the republic on the Vendée as 'genocide'. There is no doubt that executions of refractory clergy, counterrevolutionary suspects, 'brigands' and common law prisoners were enforced on a large scale. The most horrendous nocturnal slaughter was effected involving the mass drowning of captured Vendéans in the river Loire. Between 2-3000 prisoners perished in this fashion. There is no doubt that there were excesses committed by uncontrolled local terrorists. However, the royalists and the Vendéans used equally reprehensible methods and on a similar scale against captured republican forces.

Such excesses, while deplorable from a general humanitarian point of view, are inevitable in a civil war. The victory of the government forces in the Vendée was the background against which the clamour rose for the lifting of the terror. Yet the area was not completely vanquished nor were the forces of the Coalition about to abandon the field.

The Committee correctly estimated that the war was bound to re-emerge in the spring of 1794. Meanwhile, a revolutionary army of one million was being moulded, capable of defeating the revolution's enemies. Revolutionary volunteers were fused with regulars and new talented officers such as Bonaparte emerged. The latter had distinguished himself first of all as an artillery captain in the siege of Toulon. At the outset, the revolutionary army had elected officers, and representatives of the Commune or deputies on mission from the Paris Committee frequently intervened in debates on military decisions, distributed sans-culottes newspapers and harangued the soldiers in the clubs.

More than once, republican deputies such as Saint-Just were themselves architects of victory. But Carnot, in reorganising and centralising the army, considerably cut back the principle of election of officers. The ranks still elected corporals, but some of the officers achieved their position on the basis of seniority. Carnot declared on 23 December 1793: 'The armed forces do not deliberate, they obey the laws and execute them'. The clubs ceased to intervene in the administration of the army. And yet it was not coercion or the threat of the guillotine, as the slanderers of the republicans have argued, which inspired the republican *armées* of 1793-1794. They still preserved their largely democratic character, with soldiers still frequenting the clubs, and with the wide distribution of patriotic newspapers within the ranks.

Moreover, the Convention promised to reserve some emigré property for soldiers and it granted pensions to the disabled and allowances to relatives of the defenders of the *patrie* (fatherland). Saint-Just had declared: 'You must not expect victory from the numbers and discipline of soldiers alone. You will secure it only through the spread of the republican spirit within the army'. With this spirit came innovation, improvisation and new military methods. Strategy was transformed by the necessity to exploit large numbers of men in battle. Possessing a greater manoeuvrability than the Coalition armies, the republican forces could use great masses in overwhelming the enemy by sheer force of numbers. These principles, first tested out by Carnot, were vindicated in a spectacular and sweeping fashion under Bonaparte later on.

Nothing was spared in order to supply the army and defeat the counter-revolution. Lefebvre comments, 'The economy of the country was nationalised to a considerable extent, either directly by the creation of state industry or indirectly through supplying raw materials and manpower, controlling production, requisitioning supplies and price controls'. Such a policy could not have been implemented without the terror which 'compelled even the most indifferent to expend some effort'. Neither passive resistance nor rife speculation could have been suppressed without the means of coercion possessed by the Committee. This did not mean, however, that the Jacobins were 'secretly' moving in the direction of communism. Even if the Jacobins had aspired to this—which they did not—the material basis for communism did not exist in France or in Europe at that stage.

Expediency dictated the measures which the Committee took. But, with the demise of the Hébertists and a scaling down of the war, the Committee moved in the opposite direction. It handed back foreign trade to the merchants at the first opportunity and refused to introduce, as the sans-culottes demanded, a further extension of the controlled economy. At the same time, the Committee engaged in a bold policy of 'social reform' in education, industry, the civil code and public assistance. Some of these remained on paper while others were incorporated later on into the laws that emerged from the revolution.

An Education Act was passed in January 1794 and, on 4 February, slavery was abolished in all France's colonies. In late February, measures were introduced into the Convention by Saint-Just, which decreed that traitors had forfeited any claim to property, and therefore their goods would be thereafter used to eliminate pauperism. On 11 May, a scheme for providing public assistance and free medical attention to the elderly and unfit and to nursing mothers and widows at an annual cost of 50 million livres was introduced.

But the turning point in Year Two of the revolution came with the victories of the Republican armies. The terror had been required to hold down the counter-revolution while the Coalition and the royalist armies held a knife to the throat of the revolution. Much has been made by hostile historians about the 'bloody' Jacobins. And yet, according to the most authoritative analyses, the 'reign of terror', up to the execution of Robespierre, probably accounted for less than 30,000 deaths, together with another 10,000 who died in prison. Most of these were executed for participation in the civil war. The revolutionary tribunal in Paris, moreover, which was to feature in the grisly tales of bourgeois writers and historians, accounted for no more than 2639 executions. And yet, as one historian has pointed out: 'Fifteen thousand to 17,000 communards were shot in May 1871; there were perhaps 40,000 executions after the liberation of France in 1944'. This 'terror'—the first directed by the bourgeois against the Parisian workers, the second arising from the outbursts of the French people against nazi collaborators—the bourgeois have no difficulty in justifying. Not so the 'terror' of the French revolution, which, as we have pointed out, arose entirely from the forcible attempts of royalist counter-revolution in consort with feudal and semi-feudal Europe to drown the revolution in blood.

The Committee, however, stepped up the terror on 22 Prairial (10 June 1794). Writing in 1935, Trotsky said:

> Frederick Engels, who justified the terror of the Jacobins against the counter-revolution, nevertheless pointed out that: 'Once the frontiers had been safeguarded, thanks to military victories, and after the destruction of the "frenzied" Commune . . . terror outlived itself as a weapon of the revolution'. Robespierre was at the height of his powers but, says Engels, 'Henceforth terror became a means of self-preservation for him and thus it was reduced to an absurdity'.

The 'great terror' which arose from the law of 22 Prairial (10 June 1794) accounted for 1367 persons guillotined, while only 1251 had been executed in Paris from March 1793 to 10 June 1794. The revulsion arising from this, and more importantly the victory of the republican armies at Fleurus on 26 June, snapped the links between the deputies of the Plain and Robespierre. The 22 Prairial law had been introduced ostensibly to speed up the process of justice following the attempt on Robespierre's life just before. However, it deprived the prisoner of the aid of defending counsel and sent a shudder of horror and fear throughout the Convention.

With the eviction of the coalition armies from French soil, powerful tendencies developed for the dismantling of the revolutionary machinery. This was not restricted just to those who wished to see the return of the *ancien regime*. Many others, while remaining faithful to the revolution in principle, were weary and yearned for peace. The Jacobin Clubs were split down the middle and were locked in almost perpetual disagreement. The sans-culottes were alienated and showed their opposition to the Committee in many ways. The bourgeoisie in the Convention, now that the external danger was removed, wanted a rapid dismantling of the 'controlled economy' and full political and social authority for its class.

Since the break between the Jacobins and the sans-culottes, the Convention felt that it could now assert itself. As we have seen, the Jacobins never had a majority in the Convention but ruled with the compliance of the Plain. The latter for their part were prepared to tolerate the Montagnards' dictatorship so long as this was necessary to secure the revolution. It had ratified the decrees of the Committee, renewed on a monthly basis, only as long as the war danger persisted. Nevertheless, it had never forgiven the Montagnards either for having come to power on the backs of the sans-culottes or for the decimation of the Assembly. At the same time, the 22 Prairial had alarmed many of the deputies themselves. They perceived a danger to themselves if the terror continued. Disputes also broke out within the Committee of Public Safety and between that Committee and the Committee of General Security.

Carnot and Saint-Just had argued over the conduct of military operations. The 'practical men', Carnot, Lindet, etc, clashed more and more with the 'ideologues', Robespierre, Couthon and Saint-Just, whom they accused of leaning towards the sans-culottes. Robespierre also clashed with the 'terrorists' in the Committee, Billaud and Collot, who did in fact lean towards the sans-culottes. Such were the mutual hostilities and suspicions that, in the month leading up to his eventual overthrow, Robespierre withdrew in disgust from all meetings.

Thermidor

THERE HAVE BEEN endless attempts by shallow historians to explain Robespierre's downfall. This they attribute to 'issues' such as his style of dress, which is alleged to have alienated the 'dishevelled' sans-culottes, or in his imperious manner. Trotsky comments in this respect:

> The stages of the revolution and counter-revolution succeeded one another at an accelerated pace, the contradictions between the protagonists of a certain programme and the changed situation acquired an unexpected and extremely acute character. That gives the historian the possibility of displaying his retrospective wisdom by enumerating and cataloguing the mistakes, omissions, ineptness. But unfortunately, these historians abstain from indicating the right road which would have been able to lead a moderate to victory in a period of revolutionary upswing, or on the contrary to indicate a reasonable and triumphant revolutionary policy in a Thermidorean period.

In these words, Trotsky demonstrates that it was not the weaknesses or mistakes of Robespierre and his supporters, but the changed objective situation following the victory at Fleurus in particular which was the reason for his overthrow. However, while the objective situation was decisive, certain measures of the Committee, as we have seen, alienated the sans-culottes.

The Paris Commune, stuffed with supporters of Robespierre, decided at long last on 23 July to publish the new rates of wages which would operate on the basis of the amended maximum. This caused outrage amongst the Parisian workers and was hardly calculated to bind them to the Robespierre administration. The Paris Commune, at the very moment when the Convention was about to unseat Robespierre on 9 Thermidor (27 July), was preparing a military force to keep the workers in check. Despite the offer of his opponents in the Committee, led by the mediator.

Barère, for a reconciliation, Robespierre, on 8 Thermidor (26 July 1794), denounced his opponents and called for the removal of a small group of 'impure men'. At first, the Assembly voted that his speech be printed and transmitted to the municipalities. But when he was called upon to name these 'impures', he refused and therefore the Plain, fearing that Robespierre wished to have a blank cheque to continue the terror, voted to reverse its decision.

The next day when, Robespierre and Saint-Just attempted to speak to the Convention, they were shouted down. An alliance of 'moderate' Jacobins, the Plain and also 'terrorists' had united in a common fear of the Robespierrists. During the night of 8 Thermidor, they had planned with military precision, whereas Robespierre and Saint-Just were relying on their powers of oratory to sway the Convention. As soon as Robespierre stood up, his speech was drowned with cries of 'Down with the tyrant'. Saint-Just was similarly shouted down, and, on the afternoon of 9 Thermidor, the arrest of Robespierre and his main associates was ordered. Yet, Robespierre and his supporters still enjoyed huge authority in the Commune and the Paris Sections. Both the Jacobin Club and the Commune voiced support for the arrested men. Hanriot, Robespierrist chief of the National Guard, escaped from the squad sent to arrest him. The turnkey of the prison to which Robespierre and Saint-Just were sent refused to acknowledge the mandate of their escort. They were freed, to seek refuge amongst their friends in the Commune. And yet, despite their considerable advantages and the forces at their disposal, Robespierre and the Commune were defeated.

On the surface, the balance of forces seemed to be weighted in favour of the Robespierrists. The National Guard was under the same commander, which in June 1793 had forced the Convention to submit and accept the Montagnards' dictatorship. And yet, after a few hours, this force was to abandon the Commune and the Jacobin leaders, and rally to their enemies in the Convention. There was bungling on the part of Hanriot, and both Robespierre and Saint-Just demonstrated a lack of will and decisiveness. However, the critical factor in the whole episode was that the Jacobin leaders had lost the support of the Parisian sans-culottes. It is true that a force of 3000 men with 30 cannon were assembled in the Place de Grève at 7 o'clock ready to defend the Robespierrists. Yet, they lacked leaders and were reluctant to take the offensive against the Convention. The Convention in turn outlawed the accused and the rebels, at the same time intimidating the revolutionary committees and the Sections. The Jacobins deliberated, but reached no decision. Robespierre and Saint-Just were actually free and arrived at the Hôtel de Ville, but did not take charge or organise for an insurrection. As Lefebvre comments, 'They did not disavow it [the plans for an insurrection], but they probably felt that it was hopeless. Having always declared that they were governing in the name of the national representation, they were paralysed by the contradiction, and abandoned themselves to their fate'.

Gradually, the sans-culottes melted away and in the early hours of 10 Thermidor (28 July) a force of 6000 men under the control of Barras appeared in the city hall and, on behalf of the Convention, re-arrested the Robespierrists. The bourgeois Sections in the west of Paris—Tuileries, Champs Elysées, République (Roule), Louvre, Révolutionnaire (Pont Neuf), and even Piques (Robespierre's own Section) rapidly declared for the Convention. But it was equally striking that some of the most radical Sections such as Quinze Vingts, Unité, and Maison Commune supported the Convention. Moreover, the Gravilliers Section which had not forgotten Jacques Roux and thereby hated Robespierre despatched a column to support the Convention. Even Babeuf at first welcomed the overthrow of the Robespierrists and was sympathetic to the Thermidoreans. He was to regret this, along with many of the sans-culottes, later on.

During the night of 9 Thermidor, 39 of the Sections were in permanent session—and yet 35 declared unequivocally for the Convention, with only two holding out to the end for Robespierre. The mass of the workers of Paris remained largely hostile or indifferent to the pleas of Hanriot and others for a rising to defend their 'protector' and 'father'. As one report explained: 'The workers listened to him for a moment, shout "Long live the republic" and go back to their work'. Moreover, when the councillors of the Commune, two days after Robespierre's execution, were being trundled through the streets of Paris to meet the same fate, workers were reported to have shouted as they passed, 'To hell with the maximum'.

Such was the alienation of the sans-culottes that many had come to believe that the removal of Robespierre would actually mean the end of the maximum. This would in turn, they believed, end the limitation of wages, thereby restoring their living standards. Robespierre, when he realised that all was lost, attempted to shoot himself but only succeeded in shattering his jaw. He was arrested in the Hôtel de Ville without a shot being fired, and a huge round-up of the Commune members and Jacobins then ensued. On 10 Thermidor, Robespierre and Saint-Just, with 18 others, were guillotined in the Place de la Révolution.

The next day the largest batch of the whole revolution, 71 in total, were guillotined. Thus ended the Montagnards' dictatorship which had lasted from 26 July 1793, for just over a year, until 10 Thermidor (28 July 1794). Robespierre, the most hated of all the figures of the revolution as far as bourgeois historians are concerned, was nevertheless the figure that best embodied the needs of historic progress. It was not the cowardly big bourgeois, but the Jacobin dictatorship, raised on the backs of the heroic sans-culottes of Paris, which had purged France of all the feudal rubbish and secured the victory of the revolution in 1793-94. Robespierre was one of the towering figures of the eighteenth century, as Cromwell had been in the seventeenth century. The selfless devotion of the lawyer from Arras—described by Carlyle as the 'sea-green incorruptible'—died a poor man, leaving just one hundred pounds in his estate.

The curve of revolution declines

Robespierre and his friends were not just killed—they were slandered and vilified by the Thermidoreans. They were pictured as 'royalists and as men who had sold themselves to foreigners'. Thermidor reflected a deep-going rearrangement of class forces that had taken place. At the top, the Thermidoreans themselves believed that little had changed, that a few 'intransigents' had been removed. Yet, it was the pressure of the possessing classes, first of all on the Jacobins themselves, which was reflected in Thermidor. They wished above all to enjoy the fruits of their property. They exerted pressure on the state aparatus and on the Jacobin Clubs, many of whom also felt themselves to be property owners, upholders of 'order'. The Jacobin party was forced to regroup, to advance those who were swimming with the new stream and to link up with those, not of Jacobin origin, who reflected the new situation. At the same time, those who reflected the interests and passions of the urban masses were struck down. Trotsky comments:

> The first shift of power was expressed in the movement within the same old ruling party: some Jacobins forced out others. But that too was—to use Lenin's words—a stepping stone, a bridge, a rung on the ladder, upon which later the big bourgeoisie, headed by Bonaparte, was to step into power.

Following Robespierre's execution, the curve of revolution moved downwards. The Thermidoreans represented reaction, but it was a reaction on the basis of the gains of the revolution itself. Analogies can be and were drawn by Trotsky at one stage between the Thermidorean period of the French revolution and the Stalinist counter-revolution in Russia. The development of the Stalinist one-party totalitarian regime in Russia was separated by a river of blood from the heroic period of the Bolsheviks under Lenin and Trotsky between 1917 and 1923. Nevertheless, the Stalinist bureaucracy rested on the foundations of the planned economy, the main conquest of the Russian revolution. Stalin slaughtered those who made the Russian revolution and annihilated the Bolshevik Party itself. In the same way, the Thermidoreans, having despatched Robespierre and his supporters, sought to secure the power of the bourgeoisie by attacking the sans culottes and the gains which had accrued to them through the revolution.

Thermidor in power

Thermidor seemed to unwind the film of revolution. But the film did not go back to the beginning. It did not end up with a return to the *ancien regime*. In the same way as in the period of the upswing of the revolution, so in the downswing, new periods of dual power, of unstable equilibrium between different class forces, were established, not 'peacefully', but by means of civil war. Thus, the counter-revolution, clearly delineated under Thermidor, and largely at the expense of the sans-culottes, in turn resulted in the insurrections of 12 Germinal and 1-4 of Prairial in Year Three of the revolution (1 April and 20-23 May 1795). This represented a rearguard and heroic effort on the part of the Parisian sans-culottes to re-assert themselves. But it would result in their final demise as an effective political force. A popular movement, this time an avowedly proletarian movement, was not to arise until the next round of revolutions in the nineteenth century, beginning in 1830. And yet, at the outset, the former Jacobins who collaborated with the Thermidoreans believed that the removal of Robespierre was a little local difficulty, 'a partial commotion that left the government intact' (Barère). Yet the forces which the Thermidoreans had unleashed meant a sharp swing towards the right.

Rudé correctly described the Thermidorean regime as the 'Republic of proprietors', the backbone of which were those who had grown rich and powerful through the revolution. The heterogeneous coalition which had been united on 9 and 10 Thermidor by its hostility to Robespierre presented a confused picture in the beginning. The former members of the Committee of Public Safety wished to retain their power, shorn of the Robespierrist group. But the Plain was to have none of that. As early as 29 July 1794, it decreed that a fourth of each committee should be renewed, and that no member be reelected, after an interval of one month. The apparatus of revolutionary government was rapidly dismantled with the revolutionary tribunal no longer functioning and the large scale release of suspects.

Within one month, most of the Jacobins were dismissed from the Committee and one year later they were on their way to Devil's Island as 'terrorists'. Carnot, because of his specialist qualities as a military leader, was retained, and former ex-Jacobin terrorists such as Tallien, Barras and the notorious renegade Fréron moved to the right and began attacking their former allies. Fréron organised the notorious *jeunesse dorée* ('gilded' or 'golden youth'). The ranks of this reactionary scum were filled out with armed bands of draft dodgers, deserters, shopboys, and law clerks encouraged by their employers to attack the Left. Armed with cudgels, they unleashed a reign of terror on the streets against patriots while the police stood by. The Jacobins wilted under this onslaught. Given the impotence of the Commune, the National Guard, and the demise of the revolutionary Sections, no organised opposition showed itself. While the right could mobilise at will, the sans-culottes were occupied with the daily struggle for existence. Organised mass action was possible only later by means of the *journées* (days)—mass demonstrations and petitions. The influence of the sans-culottes had been considerably weakened in the Sections through the withdrawal of the forty sous compensation attendance allowance. At the same time, the assemblies were instructed to meet only once every ten days. The 48 revolutionary committees which previously existed were grouped into 12 *comités d'arrondissement* from which all Jacobin militants were excluded. Merchants, civil servants and professional men held sway in these truncated committees. The Thermidoreans also further amended the maximum legislation in order to allow prices to rise. What terror remained was directed almost entirely against the former supporters of the Mountain. The *jeunesse dorée* (sometimes called Muscadins) ruled the streets of Paris and, with their bourgeois sponsors, controlled the Sections which they had revived. There were denunciations of Jacobins, intimidation and beatings but little bloodshed in Paris. This was not the case however in the provinces. There a white terror was unleashed and frenzied bands of the 'Companies of Jesus' and the 'Companies of the Sun' hunted patriots 'as though they were partridges'. However, 'the hard faced men who had done well out of the war', the real backbone of the Thermidoreans, above all detested the controlled economy. It was their pressure which resulted in the amending of the maximum in October, which allowed prices to be raised to a level of two-thirds above that of June 1790.

However, this was not enough for the bourgeoisie, and their pressure resulted in the complete abolition of the *maximum général* in December 1794. Even before this, however, the hostility of the masses to the government grew. This took the form of a sullen resentment which police reports commented on: 'Complaints and rumours are continually heard. The long delays in obtaining rationed bread, the shortage of flour, the high prices of bread, firewood, wine, coal, vegetables and potatoes, the price of which is increasing daily in the most alarming manner, are plunging the people into a state of wretchedness and despair that is easy to imagine'.

For the first time since the autumn of 1791, the price of bread became a major social problem. While prices soared, the real wages of the Parisian workers in early 1795 were far lower than in 1793-94. It has been estimated that they 'had probably fallen back to the catastrophic level of the early months of 1789'.

The national arms factories were run down, finally being closed on 8 February 1795. Lefebvre comments: 'The debacle was so swift that economic life seemed to come to a standstill. Wages, of course, were unable to keep up with rising prices, and the constriction of markets owing to reduced purchasing power, resulted in a stoppage of production. At Littry, for example, the mines suspended operations'. Famine conditions existed in many areas of the country, with the peasants refusing to bring produce to the towns because they would not accept assignats. The government itself was reduced almost to a state of impotence. Its attempt to mollify the right threatened the very gains of the revolution. Thus, in the Vendée, rebels were offered an amnesty, the restoration of their property, exemption from military service, freedom of worship and the right to regain their arms and to police their own territory.   The consequence of this was to spread the influence of the Chouans (named after Jean Chouan, Vendée peasant leader) into most of Normandy and the virtual abandonment by the revolutionary government of the country districts of the north west of France. The counter-revolution appeared to go unchecked in the winter of 1794-95. Assassins of republicans were freed in Lyons, and royalist terrorists began to organise prison massacres just as brutal, if not on so extensive a scale, as those in Paris in September 1792. According to Lefebvre, 'By the end of spring, the Thermidoreans were no longer refusing anything, even to avowed royalists'.

The sans-culottes rise once more

The frightful conditions of the masses contrasted with the obscene wealth flaunted by the new rich in Paris. The salons revived. Extravagant new fashions displayed by the *incroyables* and the *merveilleuses* rivalled the obscene splendour of the aristocracy and the court before the revolution. Families of guillotined royalists entertained each other with the napes of their necks shorn ready for the guillotine and a thin band of red silk round their throats. Starvation for the poor on the one hand and, on the other, luxurious sumptuousness for those who could afford goods at inflated prices. This was the background against which the sans-culottes rose once more in early 1795.

At this time, one worker was heard to declare: 'As for the merchants, they were pigs fit to be killed'. In desperation, some were seduced by royalist propaganda. One worker assembling at the Tuileries in January 1795 declared: 'The devil take the republic! We are lacking everything, it is only the rich who lack nothing'. The rumours abounded that the Faubourg Saint-Antoine was once more to march on the Convention, with voices demanding that the Assembly be dispersed. Although the Jacobins had suffered from severe repression, there were some strongholds in Saint-Antoine and Saint-Marcel and the Gravilliers Section. The class hostility in early 1795 was very reminiscent of the mood that existed in Paris leading up to the Champs de Mars massacre in July 1791. It was reinforced by the closure of the remaining clubs and the arrest of local leaders— Babeuf amongst them.

The near famine conditions was the background against which the desperate uprising of the sans-culottes took place on 12 Germinal, Year Three (1 April 1795). It was the failure of the bread ration in the last two weeks of March which was the trigger for the masses to come out once more. Women stormed bakers' shops, workers, including building workers, protested. This culminated in a march on the Convention. Converging from different parts of Paris, with Saint-Marcel and the Gravilliers Section once more in the lead, an insurgent band of men and women broke into the assembly shouting, 'Bread, bread' with some wearing on their caps the slogan, 'Bread and the constitution of 1793'.   Not only was there hostility from the Thermidoreans and the Plain, but even the Mountain deputies offered them little support. The experiences of the revolution had taught them class discipline and all sections of the bourgeoisie, from the Republicans to partisans of the old regime, united in hostility to the popular movement. The insurgents were leaderless. The Paris Commune, the clubs and the Sections were either impotent or in the hands of the Thermidoreans. Moreover, the flower of republican youth were in the army. The insurgents were therefore dispersed by a force of National Guards backed up by detachments of the *jeunesse dorée*. This was the signal for a new reign of terror and the settling of old scores. Former leading Jacobins were sentenced to the 'dry guillotine', deportation to French Guiana. Even some former Jacobins who collaborated in the establishment of Thermidor were forced to flee.

However, the full weight of repression naturally fell on the shoulders of the Parisian sans-culottes. Paris was declared to be in a state of siege, and the leaders of the Germinal uprising arrested. The Sections, dominated by the *jeunesse dorée* and the bourgeoisie, pressurised the assembly on 10 April to disarm all who played a leading part in the terror. This effectively resulted in dismissal from public employment and the withdrawal of the passports of sans culottes. A minimum of 1600 were thus affected in the Paris region alone. A wave of terror was once more unleashed in the provinces. But the underlying economic difficulties and therefore the food shortages and disorders continued throughout the country. The desperation of the Parisian masses forced many to look back wistfully to the epoch of Robespierre and the Jacobin dictatorship.

An observer at the time records the views of the sans-culottes: 'Everyone was better off under the reign of Robespierre; one was then not hard pressed and needy'. A woman referring to the same period comments that, 'She missed the days of the guillotine, and that she wished that it had been permanent'. The Convention attempted, it is true, to combine repression with some minor concessions. Thus on 2 April the bread ration was to be supplemented with rice and biscuits, with priority being given to distribution to workers. However, this did not solve the question of supplies and during May and April, terrible hunger and suffering were witnessed in the streets of Paris. The numbers of beggars multiplied, people died in the streets like flies and suicides were common.

The revolt of May 1795

The mood was one of resignation and despair but with occasional outbursts of militancy. Remarkably, despite the repression and because of the continuing hunger, after a short lull the movement began again in April. Women, workers and some of the Sections such as Montreuil agitated for an increase in the food ration throughout April and early May. When the food ration fell to two ounces per head on 16 May, even the police agents warned about the possibility of an insurrection. It was the Faubourg Saint-Antoine which threatened another march on the Convention unless the food ration was increased. Pamphlets and manifestos were distributed amongst the proletariat calling for an insurrection. On 20 May (1 Prairial), the tocsin was once more sounded in the Faubourg Saint-Antoine, and again it was the women who took the lead—drawing the men behind them. They called the men out of the workshops at seven in the morning. They organised assemblies outside the bakers' shops, and compelled queuing housewives to join them in the march on the Convention. In some areas, women broke into meetings of the civil committee and demanded that their leaders put themselves at the head of a march to the Tuileries.

One outraged bourgeois, observing the action of the women, commented that 'it wasn't for women to make the laws'. The women of the Faubourg Saint-Antoine forced shops to close and led groups of armed workers in a march on the Tuileries. Along the way they forced women in shops, in private houses and even those riding in carriages to join them! On their bonnets was once again pinned the slogan, 'Bread and the constitution of 1793'. They burst into the Convention hall but were quickly ejected, only to return later with armed groups of National Guards in support of them. The detachment of sans-culottes from Saint-Antoine was headed by Guillaume Delorme, a West Indian captain of gunners, where a slave revolution led by the heroic Toussaint L'Ouverture had broken out.

This revolt of Prairial, one of the most stubborn and remarkable of the whole of the revolution, was a social protest against hunger and the hatred of the new rich. It developed over a period of four days and appeared at first as though the sans-culottes would be able to impose themselves on the Assembly. Unlike the movement in Germinal, the massive invasion by housewives and women supported by the armed battalions of the central districts and the Faubourgs, first of all cowed the Assembly. They were forced to listen as the insurgents read out their demands to the Assembly, which this time were supported by some of the deputies of the Mountain. Moreover, in the Faubourg Saint-Antoine, government troops were won over to the side of the insurgents and the city hall was captured. There was an attempt to take over and reform the Paris Commune. The Convention was surrounded and threatened as in June 1793. Yet, the sans-culottes spent hours in endless discussion, were bought off with promises, and failed to carry the insurrection to its conclusion. When they retired to their homes for the night, a force of 20,000 regular troops surrounded the Faubourg Saint-Antoine. By 23 May, it found itself isolated. The government threatened to proclaim the Faubourg in a state of rebellion and to use the troops if it failed to lay down its arms. With no support forthcoming from the rest of Paris, Saint-Antoine collapsed and with it the insurrection. This was a decisive turning point in the revolution.

Reaction and repression

The popular phase of the revolution was effectively over. Lefebvre comments: 'This is the date that should be taken as the end of the revolution. Its main spring was now broken'. The repression which followed the Germinal uprising was mild to what followed in the aftermath of Prairial. It was savage and thorough. A military commission was employed for the first time against Parisian revolutionaries. 149 were condemned to death including six Jacobin deputies. 1200 were arrested and 1700 disarmed in a single week in a savage witch-hunt against the sans-culottes. As Rudé says: 'The Parisian sans-culottes ceased to exist as a political and military force . . . From now on, the bourgeoisie, the "notables" . . . could proceed with their work without the embarrassing intervention of their one time allies'.

The heroic but doomed uprising of the Parisian masses in April and May 1795 was to leave its indelible imprint on history and was to inspire future generations. Now, however, terror against the sans culottes and the remnants of the Jacobins went hand in hand with further concessions to the right. Thus, the Convention restored the property of those who had been sentenced to death or deported, suppressed the revolutionary tribunal and pardoned the federalists. It returned the churches to the faithful while insisting that clerics take an oath of submission to the laws. In the wake of the repression against the Jacobins, a royalist resurgence naturally developed. The monarchists openly proclaimed their hopes for a restoration of the king, named members of the Convention who were ready to come to terms with them and agitated for the return of the old regime. The Count of Provence, now in Verona, took the title of Louis XVIII and, on 24 June 1795, issued a manifesto that promised punishment of the revolutionaries and the restoration of the old order.

The royalists were planning another civil war as a prelude to foreign invasion. Once more, the Chouans took up arms and looked towards an invasion by the English forces. The deputies of the

Plain, solid representatives of the bourgeoisie who had gained most through the revolution, were alarmed. They sanctioned action against royalist 'counter-terrorists' in Lyons, and Jacobins were released. The south was intimidated and an attempted royalist landing at Quiberon on 27 June capitulated to the republican General Hoche. Seven hundred and eighteen emigrés including former royalist officers were shot. The Thermidoreans, faced with this royalist threat, swung once more to the left. Royalist journalists were persecuted and arrested, while the republican press was subsidised -it was the turn of the *jeunesse dorée* to face repression at the hands of soldiers and the sans culottes. Young bourgeois draft dodgers were mercilessly pursued.

However, this was accompanied by further blows at the surviving Montagnards. They were excluded from elections. At the same time, the Thermidoreans sought to legitimise their rule through a new constitution. That of 1793, enshrining as it did the democratic rights of the people, including the right to insurrection, was anathema to the bourgeoisie. As the Prairial and Germinal uprisings had demonstrated, once the masses were on the move they would invoke the 1793 constitution as the most finished example of the democratic spirit of the revolution. It was therefore necessary to bury it once and for all. In its place, a constitution was required which would reflect the interests of the possessing classes. Boissy d'Anglas, the author of the Thermidorean constitution, declared:

> We should be governed by the best ... those who are the most educated and the most interested in maintaining the laws. With few exceptions, you will find such men only among those who, owning property, are attached to the country in which it is located, to the laws which protect it, to the peace and order which preserve it ... A country governed by landowners is in the social order: That which is governed by non-landowners is in the state of nature.

Thus, the male adult suffrage of 1793 was abandoned and a restricted franchise along the lines of the system of indirect elections of 1791 was incorporated. However, 'active' citizens now included all Frenchmen aged 21 and paying taxes—other than priests, returned emigrés, and imprisoned 'patriots'. The right of insurrection was naturally withdrawn and bicameralism was accepted with the Assembly divided into two chambers. Such a step was now possible because, with the crushing of the royalists, a 'House of Lords' was not feared by the Thermidoreans. Therefore, they proposed a council of 500, whose members were aged 30 and above, with powers to initiate legislation, while a 'council of ancients' would transform the resolutions of the lower chamber into laws. The government was to be made up of five directors (the Directory), each holding office for five years, with the right to nominate ministers who would be responsible only to it.

The Thermidoreans took measures against both the counter-revolutionaries and the Jacobins. Fearing further coordinated action in the capital, to take the place of the Commune and its mayor, they divided Paris into a number of municipalities. The clubs were once more authorised to meet, but transformed into simple public gatherings.

The constitution was, in effect, a thinly veiled dictatorship of the Directory, which gave itself the right to arrest anyone suspected of conspiracy, without the intervention of legal procedures. The laws against emigrés and priests were retained against royalist counter-revolution with relatives of emigrés barred from holding office. In order to counter any danger of a royalist upsurge, two-thirds of the deputies were to be elected from the existing Assembly—in other words, from the ranks of the Thermidoreans themselves. This blatant manoeuvre caused outrage.

The mass of the population was by now completely alienated from the Thermidorean controlled Convention. They were reduced to a frightful state. Inflation was raging ahead. In the year following the abolition of the maximum, the paper currency had increased from 8 billion to 20 billion assignats. At the same time, the poor harvest in many regions meant a shortage of food. Consequently the price of bread rocketed upwards and meat became virtually unobtainable. Government reports indicate the state of suffering of all layers of the population:

> The worker's wage is far too low to meet his daily needs; the unfortunate rentier, in order to keep alive, has to sell his last stick of furniture, which adds to the haul of the greedy speculators; the proprietor, lacking other means of subsistence, eats up his capital as well as his income; the civil servant, who is entirely dependent on his salary, also suffers the torments of privation.

In fact, the petit bourgeois layers were relatively worse off than the workers. Therefore, a ready audience for the growing royalist agitation in the city was to be found amongst this layer. Even amongst the starving and alienated sans-culottes a layer, albeit a minority, denounced the republic and looked towards the restoration of the monarchy for salvation. Citizens in the Faubourg Saint-Antoine in July 1795 were overheard to say that they did not care if the enemy came to Paris, 'because being unable to cope with high prices, it mattered little to them whether they were English or French'. However, the majority of the sans-culottes harked back to the regime of Robespierre and the controlled economy. Jacobin agitation began to revive and there was even talk of a new uprising. Commenting on the mood of the sans-culottes an observer noted in June, 'People in queues and crowds are saying that everyone thinks the workers are quiet because they have been disarmed. But they will be quite capable of using the same means to procure the bread as they did in the beginnings of the revolution'.

Robespierre under arrest following his failed suicide attempt

The Beginnings of Communism

IT WAS AGAINST a background of growing discontent on all sides that a royalist uprising—on 13 Vendémiaire (5 October 1795)—came near to overthrowing the Thermidorean Convention. The primary assemblies—in Paris they were the general assemblies of the Sections themselves—had been convened in June 1795. These meetings were to approve or reject the constitution and to appoint 'electors' who would in turn appoint deputies to the new revolutionary assembly due to meet in the Autumn of 1795. Exploiting the discontent with the Convention, royalist agitation was having a big effect, not just in the countryside, but in Paris and the provincial towns. An enormous majority of 1,057,390 to 49,788 voted for the new draft constitution.

However, the proposal for 'two-thirds' of the new deputies to be automatically elected from the previous Convention met with an entirely different reception. The Parisian Sections to whom the proposals were submitted had undergone vast changes under Thermidor. All Jacobins had been driven off the committees and even from the general meetings. The workers and the sans-culottes had been pushed aside in the Sections by the bourgeoisie and the upper petit bourgeoisie. One observer commented: 'There is only a small number of workers present at the assembly'. Thus the Sections accurately personified the 'Republic of the proprietors'. Flushed with confidence, its philosophy was summed up in the French *Gazette*: 'In all civilised communities, the proprietors alone comprise society. The others are only proletarians who, assigned to the class of supernumerary [superfluous] citizens, await the moment that will permit them to acquire property'.

The royalists controlled only one Section—Lepeletier, in the financial sector. But it was not difficult to persuade the bourgeoisie who dominated the assemblies that the Thermidoreans were violating the rights of the electors. The Thermidoreans had been given due warning of what was coming when a premature royalist insurrection broke out on 17 September 1795. The Convention replied by confirming the decree against *emigrés* and the refractory clergy. It voted for a law to control religion—forcing priests to recognise the sovereignty of the people—and established penalties against all those who attacked the sale of national property or who advocated the re-establishment of the monarchy. Worse from the big bourgeoisie's point of view was that it lifted the laws against 'terrorists', allowed them to arm and to attend the assemblies. Troops were also drafted into the capital.

These measures sparked off an explosion which led to the royalist insurrection. The royalists were in the leadership, but the majority who were involved would have rejected the ultimate aim of the restoration of the monarchy had this openly been proclaimed. The bourgeoisie was driven into the hands of the royalists by outrage at the dictatorial methods of the Thermidoreans, combined with the fear of a return of 'revolutionary government'. Throughout September, using their base in Lepeletier, the royalists began to organise throughout the Parisian Sections. By the middle of the month, they had managed to win 30 of the Sections for an address to the citizens of Paris.

On 23 September, the results of the voting in the primary assemblies were announced. This showed a vote of 205,498 in favour of the 'two-thirds', with 108,754 against. The Convention then proposed that the primary assemblies disband, the electoral assemblies be convened and the new Legislative Assembly meet in early November. But a number of the Parisian assemblies cried 'Foul'. There was a widespread belief that the vote had been rigged on a big scale. They therefore ignored the instruction to disband. At the same time, the 'gilded youth' rallied to the royalists, coming to blows with the army and ordinary citizens. They stormed through Paris declaring, 'Down with the two-thirds! Long live the king! Down with the Convention! Down with the bayonets!'.

Physical clashes developed in the Sections in late September, with the Jacobins denouncing the 'brigands' who had taken them over. Led by Lepeletier, 15 sections declared on 2 October that they were in a 'state of rebellion' against the Convention. This was the beginning of the reactionary Vendémiaire insurrection. The government countered by assembling an army of 1500 volunteers, which included some sans-culottes who had been disarmed after the Prairial uprising. Despite intense royalist agitation, raging inflation and food shortages, the sans-culottes and workers instinctively opposed the uprising and drew closer to the Convention. The big majority were not prepared to see the liquidation of the revolution, which would have quickly followed the victory of the Vendémiaire uprising. In the Champs Elysées, workers manning the local fire pumps locked the royalist sectionnaires out of their meeting place and threatened the bourgeois electors that if they joined the rebels, 'They (the workers) would set them straight'.

On 2 October, government troops under General Menou, who commanded the military forces in Paris but who had royalist leanings, were ordered to surround the headquarters of the Lepeletier Section. This they did, but Menou then negotiated with the rebels and allowed them to return to their homes. Encouraged, they prepared to mobilise 25,000 sectionnaires under arms to march on the Convention. In the event, 7-8000 took part in the attack on the Convention. The government, however, had prepared 5000 troops under the overall command of Barras but with the young General Bonaparte, only recently on the inactive list, put in charge of artillery. Bonaparte was just one of half a dozen generals who served under Barras in this affair, and only *ex post facto*, on Barras's recommendation, was Bonaparte officially recognised as his second in command. The Tuileries was converted into an armed fortress, with 40 cannon installed and all the approaches manned. When the rebels advanced, they were met with Bonaparte's famous 'whiff of grapeshot': in fact, it was withering gunfire. With heavy casualties on both sides, the royalist rebels were eventually driven back at six o'clock in the evening. There was a minor skirmish the next day, but the Royalists had effectively been broken. The government proceeded to close down the primary assemblies, and set up military courts to try the principal authors of the rebellion. This repression was much milder than that which followed the putting down of the sans-culottes' Prairial uprising. The Thermidoreans were anxious not to drive too great a wedge between themselves and the bourgeois Sections which had supported the uprising. Therefore, the mass of the participants in Vendémiaire were considered to be mere dupes of a handful of royalists. The repression was concentrated against a small number of instigators, journalists, known royalists, presidents and secretaries of sectional assemblies. Yet, the great majority of these were allowed to escape. A mere 30 out of 200 of those originally arrested were tried by military courts. Only two were executed, eight more were acquitted and the rest were sentenced to fines or imprisonment.

However, the suppression of Vendémiaire did nothing to lighten the burden of the sans-culottes. High prices and scarcity continued with even greater increases for bread and fuel as the winter of 1795 approached. Hopelessness and despair gripped the population. An observer commented: 'Poverty is at its lowest depths; the streets

117

of Paris present the grievous spectacle of women and children on the point of collapse from lack of nourishment; the hospitals and alms houses will soon be insufficient to house the army of sick and wretched. Poverty and hunger have almost completely silenced their voices; but when on occasion their voices are raised, it is in muttered imprecations against the government'. The remnants of the Jacobins were silent, the sans-culottes militants were dispirited, scattered or imprisoned. The population was cowed by the army, brought in by the Convention but now remaining as a permanent occupying force in the capital.

The unstable equilibrium between different class forces compelled the Thermidoreans to zig-zag from left to right. But the army, and particularly the generals, were to become the ultimate arbiters of political disputes, the real power behind the facade of a 'liberal' constitution. This deadlock between different class forces was to lay the basis for the eventual coming to power on 18 Brumaire of Napoleon Bonaparte.

The Conspiracy of Equals

In the aftermath of Vendémiare, the Thermidorean regime swung to the left, accompanied by attempts to invoke the 'republican spirit'. Concessions were made to the remnants of Jacobinsm and the sans culottes. Jacobin activity began to revive and the clubs re-opened; Gracchus—he took his name from the Gracchi of ancient Rome—Babeuf restarted *Tribune du Peuple*.

Babeuf had evolved from a keeper of the manorial rolls, an agent of the feudal system and a comparatively well paid job, to become the leader of the communist 'Conspiracy of Equals'. This movement appeared in the downswing of the revolution, in the last act so to speak, and when the proletariat had been exhausted by the preceding struggles. Doomed to inevitable defeat, it is nevertheless a vital episode in the revolution, a bridge from the plebeian sans-culottes to the modern socialist and Marxist movement. Babeuf, Darthé, Buonarotti and their comrades stood for a communist organisation of society. Given the undeveloped character of the productive forces and the proletariat at that stage, it was not, nor could it have been, the communism of Marx and Engels, that is, scientific socialism. Yet it was an important and heroic first attempt to formulate, in an inevitably rather idealistic fashion, the idea of a future communistic society.

No sooner had the bourgeoisie carried through its revolution, than it was faced, in embryo, with its future 'grave diggers'. Babeuf articulated both the masses' disappointment at the results of the revolution, and the yearning of the dispossessed for a society which could solve their problems. His solution was for equality, the sharing of goods in common, and later the idea of common ownership. Babeuf began as a champion of the peasantry. He later wrote that his job as a keeper of the manorial rolls allowed him to discover 'amid the dusty archives, the repulsive secrets of the nobility and the story of its usurpation of the land of France'. During the revolution he became a firm advocate of 'agrarian law', which for him meant the abolition of private property and of the division of society into exploited and exploiters.

As early as 1791, he advocated land division as a step towards a classless society. His efforts to defend the poor, both in the rural and the urban areas, his opposition to limits on free expression of thought, speech and writing led to inevitable imprisonment. Robespierre's attempts to limit the press and free speech together with the attacks on the rights and conditions of the sans-culottes earned the opposition of Babeuf. Indeed, initially he welcomed 9 Thermidor, believing that the overthrow of Robespierre would lead to the re-introduction of the still-born constitution of 1793. His hopes disappointed, he came to oppose the Thermidoreans and this led to a further period of imprisonment. While he was incarcerated, news of the Prairial uprising reached him. He took this as evidence of the readiness of the proletariat to continue the revolutionary struggle, and he produced a special manifesto in September 1795 denouncing the new tyranny of the rich.

In prison, he met and discussed with other revolutionaries, ex-Jacobins and sans-culottes. It was at this time, in late 1795, that he was to meet Filippo Buonarotti. Intense discussion and debate amongst the revolutionaries resulted in the formulation of the ideas of 'communism', which were later to be summarised in the manifesto of the 'Conspiracy of Equals'. As has happened many times in history, the prisons became the 'universities of the revolution'.

Babeuf was released in October 1795, full of hope and determined to rally the Parisian masses. But, as he emerged from the Abbaye prison, he could not fail to notice the passivity and inertia which gripped the masses. He wondered what had become of the heroic people of the Parisian suburbs. But as Trotsky pointed out:

A revolution is a great devourer of human energy both in the individual and collective sense. The nerves give way. Consciousness is shaken and characters are worn out. Events unfold too swiftly for the flow of fresh forces to replace the loss. Hunger, unemployment, the death of the revolutionary cadres, the removal of the masses

119

from administration, all this led to such a physical and moral impoverishment of the Parisian suburbs that they required three decades before they were ready for a new insurrection.

Nevertheless, in the most difficult circumstances, in November 1795 Babeuf resumed the publication of the *Tribune du Peuple*. Together with sans-culottes friends and members of the National Convention, such as Jean Baptiste Drouet, the post master of Ste Menehould and a member of the Mountain, and ex-Jacobins like Felix Lepeletier, he set up the *Club du Panthéon*. Its purpose was to openly agitate for the overthrow of the Thermidorean dictatorship and a return to the constitution of 1793. They attracted thousands to their meetings, and the growth in their support alarmed the government. Therefore, on 27 February 1796, the Club was raided by a force commanded by Napoleon Bonaparte, who drove out the membership and barred the doors.

During the spring of 1796, the government, maintaining itself in power by the use of a vast network of spies, summary arrests, laws illegalising political opposition, and other repressive measures, drove the Panthéonists underground. In this situation was born the *Conspiration pour l'Égalité* -the Conspiracy of Equals. A directorate was set up in March 1796, amongst whom were included, apart from Babeuf himself, Buonarotti, Sylvain Maréchal, Felix le Peletier and AA Darthé. The Equals set about mobilising the sans culottes, the body of Paris militants who still remained faithful to the original ideals of the revolution, estimated by Babeuf at something like 17,000 men. By means of placards, handbills, leaflets and pamphlets, an appeal was made to the masses of Paris and the major cities to organise the people of France to overthrow the Thermidorean tyranny.

The manifesto of the Equals, written by Sylvain Maréchal, revolutionary writer and orator, took as its motto a phrase of the philospher, Condorcet—'Equality of fact, the final aim of social art'. It began with the words:

> People of France! During fifteen centuries you have lived as slaves, and in consequence unhappily. It is scarcely six years that you have begun to breathe, in the expectation of independence, happiness, equality! . . . Always and everywhere the poor human race, delivered over to more or less adroit cannibals, has served as a plaything for all ambitions, as a pasture for all tyrannies. Always and everywhere men have been lulled by fine words; never and nowhere have they obtained the thing with the word. From time immemorial it has been repeated, with hypocrisy, that men are equal and from time immemorial the most degrading and the most monstrous inequality ceaselessly weighs on the human race . . . Equality has never been

anything but a beautiful and sterile fiction of the law. Today when it is demanded with a stronger voice, they reply to us: 'Be silent, wretches! Equality of fact is nought but a chimera: be contented with conditional equality, you are all equal before the law. Canaille, what do you want more?' What do we want more? Legislators, governors, rich proprietors, listen, in your turn! We are all equal, are we not? This principle remains uncontested. For, unless attacked by madness, no-one could seriously say that it was night when it was day.

Well! We demand henceforth to live and to die equal, as we have been born equal. We demand real equality or death; that is what we want.

And we shall have it, this real equality, it matters not at what price! Woe betide those who place themselves between us and it! Woe betide him who offers resistance to a vow thus pronounced!

The French revolution is but the precursor of another, and a greater and more solemn revolution, and which will be the last! The people has marched over the bodies of kings and priests who coalesced against it: it will be the same with the new tyrants, with the new political hypocrites, seated in the place of the old ones! What do we want more than equality of rights? We want not only the equality transcribed in the Declaration of the Rights of Man and the citizen; we will have it in the midst of us, under the roof of our houses. We consent to everything for its sake; to make a clear board, that we may hold to it alone . . . .Legislators and governors, who have neither genius nor good faith; rich proprietors without bowels of compassion, you will try in vain to neutralise our holy enterprise by saying that it does no more than reproduce that agrarian law already demanded more than once before! Calumniators! Be silent in your turn and, in the silence of confusion, listen to our demands dictated by nature and based upon justice!

The agrarian law, or the partition of lands, was the immediate aim of certain soldiers without principles, of certain peoples moved by their instinct rather than by reason. We aim at something more sublime and more equitable—the common good, or the community of goods. No more individual property in land; the land belongs to no-one. We demand, we would have the communal enjoyments of the fruits of the earth, fruits which are for everyone!

We declare that we can no longer suffer with the enormous majority of men, labour and sweat in the service and for the good pleasure of a small minority! Enough and too long have less than a million of individuals disposed of that which belongs to more than twenty millions of their kind!

Let this great scandal that our grandchildren will hardly be willing to believe in, cease! Let disappear once and for all the revolting distinction of rich and poor, of great and small, of masters and valets, of governors and governed! Let there be no other differences between the human beings than those of age and sex . . . The moment has arrived for founding the Republic of the Equals, that grand refuge open for all men. The days of general restitution have come. Families groaning in misery, come and seat yourselves at the common table prepared by nature for all her children! People of France! The purest form of all glory has been reserved for thee! Yes, it is you who may first offer to the world this touching spectacle . . .

The day after this veritable revolution they will say, with astonishment, What? the common-well being was to be had for so little? We had only to will it. Ah! Why do we not will it sooner? Why had we to be told about it so many times? Yes, doubtless, with one man on earth richer, more powerful than his neighbours, than his equals, the equilibrium is broken, crime and misery are already in the world. People of France! By what sign ought you henceforward to recognise the excellence of a constitution? That which rests entirely on an equality of fact is the only one that can benefit you and satisfy all your wants.

Then the declaration clearly differentiated between the constitutions of 1791 and 1795 on the one side and 1793 on the other:

The aristocratic charters of 1791 to 1795 have only riveted your bonds instead of rending them. That of 1793 was a great step indeed towards real equality, and never before had it been approached so closely; but yet, it did not achieve the aim and did not touch the common well being, of which, nevertheless, it solemnly consecrated the great principle.

People of France! Open your eyes and your heart to the fullness of happiness. Recognise and proclaim with us the 'Republic of the Equals'.

This bold appeal found a ready audience amongst the thousands of sans-culottes in the slums and Faubourgs of Paris. One account pictures a crowd of 2000 gathered around a poster of the Equals. A troop of soldiers arrives and the officer threatens to tear down the poster. The crowd, eagerly agreeing with the sentiments expressed, restrained the officer who, on departing, agreed that the poster correctly expressed the views of the people of Paris. However, passive acceptance of Babeuf's ideas was one thing, proceeding to insurrection something entirely different. The masses cannot be turned on and off like a tap. The sans-culottes, since the failure of the Prairial uprising, were cowed and silent and refused to respond to the call of the Equals. The 'conspirators' were eventually betrayed by Grisel, a police spy who had insinuated himself into the inner circle of the Equals. He was an agent of Carnot, who was now part of the Directory, and was rapidly moving towards the right. Babeuf was to be avenged; Grisel was killed by Babeuf's son Émile in a duel some years later.

In early May, the government struck; 131, including Babeuf and most of the leaders of the conspiracy, were arrested. The Babouvists still at large attempted an insurrection, but were crushed. Thirty were summarily executed. Babeuf himself and the other leaders were imprisoned in Paris but later transported, in specially constructed cages to make them appear like wild animals, to Vendôme for trial. Nine months after they were arrested 65 defendants, some of them in absentia, were put on trial. Some futile attempts were made by the supporters of Babeuf who were still at large to free the prisoners but they failed. The high point of the trial was undoubtedly the magnificent speech of Babeuf himself before the court. At the outset he boldly declared:

> To die a martyr does not cut short a man's life; such a death, rather, confers immortality, for the man who dies in such a cause lives on in the hearts of his people.
>
> The revolution's greatest days, when it triumphed over all its enemies, when it vindicated gloriously the rights of the people, are here portrayed as harbingers of dire calamity. The end of the bigoted rule of priests is bewailed because it has led to the spread of 'atheism'. Those happy changes confidently expected as a result of the establishment of the republic are dubbed 'anarchy'. Those measures that were dictated as a means of breaking the resistance of the country's enemies are branded as chaos, murder, and robbery. Laws for the relief of misery are seen as nothing more than red ruin. Those who rally to the defence of the republic are pilloried as murderers, anarchists, evil doers, monsters newly emerged from their hidden lairs.

Babeuf indicted the Thermidoreans as usurpers and betrayers of the revolution. He stated:

> The accumulation of power and privilege in the hands of a tiny minority already rendered formidable by reason of its wealth alone, and the slavish subjection of practically the entire people to this handful of the mighty—this the prosecution calls order. But we call this disorder. Order is only thinkable to us when the entire people are free and happy.

Defending the right of insurrection against an unjust government which had been expunged from the 1795 constitution he stated:

> The greatest error in all politics is doubtless the idea that the essence of conspiracy consists in the intent to overthrow established governments. If this were true, the peoples would be doomed to remain for all time under any government, no matter how base and vile, that had once succeeded in establishing itself. Such reasoning flouts the principle of the sovereignty of the people; it is nothing more than a new version of the divine rights of kings. From this viewpoint the revolution of 14 July, 1789, which overthrew an established government, was a criminal conspiracy.

I saw, in the existing government, the sovereignty of the people slighted, and the right to elect and to be elected granted exclusively to a small minority. I saw the revival, not merely of ancient privilege, but of new and odious distinctions between active and passive citizens. I saw all the guarantees of personal freedom swept away—the right of petition and of assembly, the right of the people to bear arms, the right to a free press. What was worse, I saw the people's sacred inalienable right to make the laws taken away from them and vested in a second chamber; and this notwithstanding the fact that throughout the entire revolution the bicameral system had been so long and so bitterly opposed. At the same time I saw the executive vested with great power and removed from popular control—it was even given the power to remove the popular representatives and to replace them at its discretion. I saw social services and public education completely ignored. How different was the state of affairs before! The previous constitution had been overthrown and the present one had been established against the wishes of the people. The previous constitution had been sanctioned by 4,800,000 votes cast freely, decisively, and almost unanimously. The existing one was propped up by at most 900,000 votes, cast under the most dubious circumstances.

After 13 Vendémiaire, I became aware that the masses—weary of a revolution whose twists and turns had brought them only sorrow—had,it must be admitted, turned back to royalism. In Paris I saw that the simple and unlettered people had been led by their enemies to feel a cordial detestation for the Republic. The masses whose judgement is guided by daily experience, had with little difficulty to ask themselves: How did we fare under the crown and how is it now under the republic? In the ensuing comparison the republic came off second best . . . .I looked about me. I saw that many, many people were downhearted, yes, even many patriots were downhearted who earlier had waged so valiant and victorious a struggle for freedom. Demoralisation had spread far and wide and an absolute paralysis of popular initiative had set in. The masses had been stripped of all basic guarantees against the excesses of their rulers, and so disarmed. Our brave revolutionaries still bore the marks of their ancient chains; not a few of them, who did not think the matter through clearly, had almost come to the conclusion that the republic could not be anything so marvellous after all.

Babeuf explained that he therefore launched the 'Tribune of the People' in which he declared that the republic was:

not just a word, a meaningless phrase. The slogan of liberty and equality, which was so long dinned into your ears, had a certain charm in the early days of the revolution, because you believed that it contained real meaning. Today this slogan means nothing to you any more; it is only an empty oratorical flourish. But we must repeat again and again that this slogan, notwithstanding all our recent painful experiences, can and should connote something of a deep significance for the masses.

Anticipating elements of Trotsky's future theory of the Permanent Revolution, Babeuf then declared:

> The aim of the revolution, furthermore, is to realise the happiness of the majority. If, therefore, this aim is not fulfilled, if the people do not succeed in attaining the better life which was the object of their struggle, then the revolution is not over.

Inveighing against the rich, Babeuf quoted from the *Outline of Babeuf's doctrine* which was the main prosecution evidence:

> The purpose of the revolution is to abolish inequality and to restore the common welfare. The revolution is not yet at an end, since the wealthy have diverted its fruits, including political power, to their own exclusive use, while the poor in their toil and misery lead a life of actual slavery and count for nothing in the state.
>
> There was no question of these ideas being put into effect if the people willed otherwise. As a matter of fact, I was very far from enjoying a measure of popular support.

His following words contrast with the miserable attempts of the present leaders of the labour movement to accommodate themselves to every twist and turn of so-called 'public opinion':

> On the contrary it is only too easy to become discouraged by the difficulties and the dangers involved in taking a case to the public, and only too tempting to conclude that the enterprise is hopeless before even putting the matter to the test.

Drawing on all the great writers who inspired the French revolution such as Mably, Rousseau, Diderot and others, Babeuf comes out with a bold defence of his communistic ideas. They were bound to be of a utopian character, not really going beyond the sharing of goods in common. Given the absence of large scale industry and of a modern proletariat, Babeuf was incapable of rising to the heights of scientific socialism, the communism of Marx and Engels. And yet the tradition that he laid down in the festering slums of Paris and amongst the emerging proletariat was to be carried through to the nineteenth century from one generation to another. The heritage of Gracchus Babeuf, as with the other great utopian socialists such as St Simon, Fourier and Robert Owen, laid the foundations on which the modern labour movement and scientific socialism itself were built.

Babeuf and Darthé were found guilty by the Thermidorean court and were executed on 27 May 1797. However, their ideas lived on through those like Buonarotti who, after years of imprisonment and old age, wrote his history of the 'Conspiracy of the Equals'. This was eagerly seized upon by the proletariat in France and Europe in the first half of the nineteenth century. Engels comments:

> [Communism] was first discussed in the dark lanes and crowded alleys of the Parisian suburb, Saint-Antoine, and soon after in the secret assemblies of conspirators . . . Communist ideas spread rapidly over Paris, Lyons, Toulouse and the other large and manufacturing towns of the realm; various secret associations followed each other, and among which the *Travailleurs Égalitaires* (equalitarian workingmen), and the Humanitarians were the most considerable.
>
> The Equalitarians were rather a 'rough set', like the Babouvists of the great revolution; they proposed making the world a working man's community, putting down every refinement of civilisation, science, the fine arts, etc as useless, dangerous, and aristocratic luxuries, a prejudice necessarily arising from the total ignorance of history and political economy.

In 1843 Engels estimated that the 'French Icarian communists are estimated at about half a million in number, women and children not taken into account. A pretty respectable phalanx, isn't it?'

Thus, in cutting off the head of Babeuf and his comrades, the French bourgeoisie did not eliminate his influence. Like the bourgeoisie of other countries later, they were to learn that no amount of guillotines, guns or torture chambers can eliminate the ideas of socialism which are rooted in the very development of the proletariat as a class.

Babeuf's ideas were not at all restricted to France. They were a formative influence in the rise of Chartism in Britain, the first distinctly independent mass political movement of the working class in history. Buonarotti's history of 'Babouvism' was translated into English by the Chartist leader Bronterre O'Brien. It had a profound influence on the British proletariat, as did the French revolution as a whole. This was reflected at a meeting in 1845 in London which was addressed, amongst others, by the Chartist leader George Julian Harney. In a speech which was commented on by Engels, he dissected the various stages and the characters in the French revolution. He said of the founder of French communism:

> Babeuf was one of these, the originator of the famous conspiracy known by his name. That conspiracy had for its object the establishment of a veritable republic, in which the selfishness of individualism should be known no more—(cheers), in which private

property and money, the foundation and the root of all wrong and evil, should cease to be—(cheers); and in which the happiness of all should be based upon the common labour and equal enjoyment of all (great cheering). These glorious men pursued their glorious object to the death. Babeuf and Darthé sealed their belief with their blood, and Buonarotti, through years of imprisonment, penury and old age, persevered to the last in his advocacy of the great principles which we this night dare to vindicate. Nor should I omit mention of those heroic deputies Romme, Soubrany, Duroy, Duquesnoy and their compatriots, who, condemned to death by the traitor aristocrats of the Convention, heroically slew themselves in front of, and in contempt of their assassins, performing this self-tragedy with a single blade which they passed from hand to hand.

Jean Paul Marat, Carlyle's 'sea green incorruptible'

The Victory of Bonapartism

IN THE CONDITIONS which then obtained in France, the Conspiracy of Equals could only be a glorious anticipation of the future movement of the proletariat. The crushing of the conspiracy moved the political pendulum to the right. The royalists once more raised their heads. The mere denunciation of 'suspect' functionaries was sufficent for their removal from office, to be replaced by royalist sympathisers. Thus the royalist, Willot, was put in command of Provence, where he again permitted the 'white terror' to be unleashed. Even the guard of the Directory was discovered to be involved in a plot with the agents of Louis XVIII for the overthrow of the regime. Besieged from both right and left, the Directory faced enormous difficulties in financing the war against the coalition. This was only achieved by further sale of national property, diamonds and other valuables, quite apart from land. Loans were raised with difficulty from war contractors, who practiced corruption on a large scale. One of the directors, Barras, was widely known as an embezzler. Bond holders were cheated by the state, with peasants and others being forced to sell them to bidders at next to nothing.

The whole of the country was in a state of decay: the highways were falling apart, courts and schools were neglected by impoverished local administrations, and even the constabulary were forced to sell their horses because they could not feed them! The Directory hoped to stave off popular discontent by basking in the military victories of Napoleon Bonaparte. But they were to be cruelly disappointed in the election of April 1797. Sitting Thermidorean candidates were defeated. Only one-third of the seats were up for election, but out of a total 216, only 11 former deputies, supporters of the Thermidoreans, were returned. In an effort to exploit their victory, the right sought to cripple the Directory by taking away its power to control the government and

128

the direction of the war. If successful, this would have opened the flood gates to the Right and the eventual restoration of the monarchy. On 18 June 1797, the right managed to effect the transfer of all financial administrations from the Directory to the treasury, which was stuffed with reactionaries. The 'elders' rejected the recommendation, but the growth in support for the Right, now with a majority of royalists in their ranks, convinced most of the Directors that they must strike a decisive blow.

Enter Napoleon Bonaparte

However, there was no question of resorting to popular force. One of the Directors, La Revellière-Lépeaux, refused to sanction even the limited measures of mobilising the sans-culottes, as had been done to crush the royalist uprising during Vendémiaire. But if the Thermidorean bourgeoisie could not appeal to the people, only one reliable force remained: the army. Therefore, Bonaparte, fresh from victories in Italy, together with Hoche marched on Paris to save the Directory. During the night of 17-18 Fructidor (3 and 4 September 1797), the troops occupied the city. The royalist leaders were arrested—it was quite clear that they were preparing a new Vendémiaire uprising. Carnot, who, as a Director, had been collaborating with the royalists, fled. 214 deputies were purged from the councils, and 65 conspirators were deported to French Guiana.

Aiming its blows against right as well as left, a proclamation declared that advocates of either the monarchy or the constitution of 1793 would be shot without trial. Foreign refugees were forced to leave France, and hundreds of priests were deported or forced to take new oaths of loyalty. Throughout Fructidor, it was clear that, despite the 'liberal' constitution, the army was the real power upon which the regime ultimately rested. Bonaparte in particular, victorious in Italy and saviour of the Thermidoreans in Fructidor, saw his authority enormously enhanced.

Having crushed the right, the Directors now turned to the danger from the left. The Jacobins, in the absence of the royalists, were the main catalyst of the opposition in the elections in May 1798. However, the Thermidorean Assembly then merely passed a law excluding 106 Jacobin deputies from taking their places in the Chamber. Yet a combination of internal factors—chaotic tax collection, a fall in the price of grain as well as the continuing naval war with England—resulted in a situation of chronic instability. The Directory attempted to solve its problem by the plundering of the resources from conquered or satellite territories. Conditions were therefore laid for a further outbreak of war with the second Coalition, which this time involved Britain, Austria, Russia, Turkey and Sweden.

To begin with, the war proceeded badly for the French. Once more a 'defensive war' against European reaction resulted in a further swing to the left within the country. Despite the Directors' denunciations of both royalism and 'anarchy', two-thirds of the government's candidates in the 1799 election were defeated and the Jacobins increased their strength.

In the period after the elections, the Directory was besieged on all sides. According to a police report, 'Everything was falling apart'. One of the directors, Reubell, left the Directory, and was replaced by Sieyès, an open enemy of the Directors. This laid the basis for what was in effect the parliamentary coup d'etat on 30 Prairial (18 June 1799), with Sieyès and his supporters evicting the Directors opposed to him. Sieyès appointed as Minister of Finance, Robert Lindet, one of Robespierre's collaborators and also involved in the Babeuf conspiracy. Jacobin strength was increased, newspapers re-appeared, clubs were opened and freedom of the press re-established. Drouet, one of the leaders of the Babeuf conspiracy, was able to open the Manège Club. The influence of the Left seemed to be reaffirmed, with even echoes of the 'revolutionary government' of 1793-4. A new *levée en masse* was introduced and the National Guard was reorganised. The Jacobin revival seemed unstoppable as a repressive law of hostages was introduced whereby relatives of emigrés and rebels were interned. It was stipulated that the murder of one supporter of the regime would result in four from the Right being deported!

Summary execution was decreed for any 'rebel' possessing arms. Forced loans were decreed by the assembly and the Jacobins were pressing for a reawakening of the old revolutionary ardour amongst the people. However, the bourgeoisie, which provided the bedrock of support for the Directory and the Assembly. took fright at this. One observer at the time commented: 'Some want to employ popular force to repel the barbarians; others fear the use of this all powerful force, that is to say, they fear the mass of the republicans more than the hordes from the north'.

In the face of forced loans, the bourgeoisie in effect went on strike, with the wealthy dismissing servants and leaving Paris, while others announced the closure of factories. Clashes between the 'gilded youth' and the Jacobins and their sympathisers took place in several towns such as Rouen, Amiens, Caen and Bordeaux as well as in Paris itself. Yet the masses, discouraged since the Prairial uprising, were largely indifferent to the appeals of the Jacobins. Moreover, the bourgeoisie were alarmed at their agitation. Through the newly installed police chief Fouché, the government closed down the Jacobin Clubs. This did nothing to mollify the royalists, who organised an insurrection on 5 August 1799. At one stage, the city of Toulouse was completely surrounded. Eventually, however, the royalists were beaten back and dispersed. When this news reached Paris, Sieyès deported the staff of 34 of the remaining royalist newspapers but 'balanced' this with an order for the arrest of the staff of 16 other papers, with Jacobin publications on the list.

It was a fresh outbreak of the war which had led to the partial revival of Jacobinism. But as with the victory at Fleurus, which hastened the downfall of Robespierre, so the victory of French armies in Italy and Holland lifted the threat of invasion and in turn led to the demise once more of the Jacobins. Bonaparte had landed at Frejus and was moving towards Paris. This unleashed a wave of enthusiasm everywhere. Lefebvre comments:

> The return of the 'Invincible' finally gave the assurance that the republic was safe. Since the outset of the war the pattern had always been the same. Defeat produced extreme measures, and victory made them unnecessary. In times of danger the Jacobins won control because of their daring and intransigence. Once the danger was passed, the moderates triumphed easily, and the reaction was then consolidated.

And yet France remained chronically unstable.

The 18 Brumaire

The bourgeoisie, having completely lost confidence in their own political capacity, took refuge in the corruption of the Directory, and finally sought shelter under the wing of Napoleonic despotism. In the words of Frederick Engels, 'The promised eternal peace was turned into an endless war of conquest'. Bonapartism is a bourgeois variety of Caesarism. In essence, it is a military dictatorship, 'rule by the sword'. Such a regime is only possible when the struggle between the classes almost cancels each other out. In this situation of class deadlock, the state is able to raise itself above the classes to balance between them, only in the final analysis representing the economically dominant class in society.

The bourgeoisie had garnered the fruits of the revolution as we have seen. However, it still appeared to be menaced on all sides. It confronted the ever-present threat of royalist counter-revolution together with reactionary Europe on the one side, and the bugbear of Jacobinism on the other. For the time being, the bourgeoisie was reassured by the power which Sieyès, its political high priest, wielded within the Directory. Sieyès was, however, planning his own coup d'etat to establish a stable government. But the Assembly now possessed a republican majority, and therefore, as in 18 Fructidor, the army would have to be relied upon. Sieyès' plan involved the neutering of the Assembly and the councils. They were bound to resist, and therefore the conspirators turned towards Napoleon Bonaparte. The latter was enormously popular, had an outstanding military record and limitless ambition—and moreover had a Jacobin past which would bestow 'revolutionary' authority upon the plotters.

By banging on the 'terrorist' drum once more, they persuaded the councils to meet outside of Paris. The 'ancients' or elders (the body of 250 members which translated the resolutions of the Council of 500 into laws if appropriate) were soon won over, but the Council of 500 (the 'lower house' which merely proposed legislation) was obstinate. When Napoleon entered without being summoned, he was attacked furiously by the assembled deputies and was forced to leave the chamber with the cries of 'Outlaw him' ringing in his ears. Bonaparte then attempted to appeal to the grenadiers defending the chamber, but it was only the intervention of his brother Lucien on horseback that saved him. Lucien, denouncing the representatives as agents of England who had attacked Bonaparte with daggers, succeeded in winning them over. They in turn forced the evacuation of the 500. The Directory was dissolved, and power was vested in a provisional 'consulate' of Sieyès, Roger-Ducos and Bonaparte himself.

The consuls were supposed to be equal, but it was Bonaparte himself who emerged as the victor on 18 Brumaire. Soon he was to eclipse the two other consuls and establish a military dictatorship. Thus, ten years after the revolution, the bourgeois republic was terminated. Three weeks after 18 Brumaire, a new dictatorial constitution was implemented. At the same time, the organs of popular control and involvement, imperfect as they were under the Directory, were abolished and replaced by an administration of prefects. In the proclamation that accompanied the new 'Caesarian constitution', the consuls declared: 'The revolution is established upon the principles which began it: It is ended'. Sieyès and his supporters were prepared to lean on Bonaparte to achieve their aims—and drop him at the first convenient opportunity.

However, they had reckoned without the immense popularity of

Bonaparte and his adroit ability to manoeuvre and intrigue, which matched and even outstripped that of Sieyès himself. By playing off one group against another, Bonaparte achieved the acceptance of a constitution which, while retaining the Senate and Tribunate (with reduced legislative initiative), designated a first consul who was to be elected for ten years, with powers to overrule the other consuls. Naturally, this first consul would be Bonaparte himself.

The constitution was put to a plebiscite, which henceforth became a typical method of Bonapartism, and was overwhelmingly accepted in February 1800. Sieyès and his supporters believed that they would still be able to use the Tribunate and Legislature to check Napoleon. But Bonaparte ruled without it and often against it through a Council of State made up of the most experienced legislators. Gradually, he elbowed all his opponents aside, becoming, by means of another plebiscite, a Consul for Life.

This was followed in 1802 with an amended constitution which gave him virtually complete dictatorial powers. Finally, he was crowned emperor, receiving the blessing of the Pope in Notre Dame Cathedral in December 1804. Under Napoleon, the great work undertaken in progressive legislation during the revolution was consolidated. The greatest achievement was perhaps the *Code Civil*, a perfect expression of juridical relations corresponding to the rule of the bourgeoisie. As Frederick Engels pointed out, it was 'so masterly that this French revolutionary code still serves as a model for reforms for the law of property in all other countries, not excepting England'. The Code preserved the legal egalitarian principles of 1789, but sharply insisted on the rights of property and on the 'authority' of parent and husband. The democratic principles of 1793 were rejected of course. But the destruction of feudalism and feudal privileges were endorsed as were, rather hypocritically, liberty of conscience and employment.

Reflecting the views of the bourgeoisie, the rights of women were curtailed, with divorce severely restricted and almost impossible for a wronged wife. One clause read, 'A husband owes protection to his wife, a wife obedience to her husband . . . Married women are incapable of making contracts'.

The restrictions against the trade unions embodied in the Le Chapelier laws were reinforced by a ban in 1803 which outlawed unions and forced workers to carry a pass book stamped by their employer. In the sphere of religion, Bonaparte was sceptical, but, like his former mentor Robespierre, considered that it was necessary to use religion to keep the masses in check. He wrote 'In religion I do not see the mystery of the incarnation, but the mystery of the social order'. He stated further, 'Society is impossible without inequality, inequality is intolerable without a code of morality, and a code of morality unacceptable without religion'.

The Napoleonic wars

On the one hand, the regime of Bonapartism represented reaction compared to the heroic period of the revolution. But as against the rest of feudal and semi-feudal Europe, Bonaparte's regime represented a mortal threat. Despite his jettisoning of his earlier Jacobin past, his ascendency to the throne and his embracing of the Catholic religion, he nevertheless was an object of hatred to the whole of reactionary Europe because he rested on and defended the property system which had issued from the revolution. Therefore, a resumption of war with the Coalition was inevitable. This broke out in 1803 and was to stretch right up to the overthrow of Napoleon himself in 1815.

A brilliant strategist and improviser, under his leadership and that of the new generals who had emerged because of the revolution, the French armies carried the bourgeois revolution to the rest of Europe. Marx and Engels commented in *The Holy Family* that Napoleon 'Perfected the terror by substituting permanent war for permanent revolution'. He tore up by the roots the old regime in parts of Europe and introduced equality before the law, civil marriage, secular education, the abolition of privileges, corporate bodies, tithes and feudal views. However, at no time did the French army invoke the example of 1793, and it was not the sans-culottes or the small peasants in the countries occupied but the bourgeoisie who would benefit from the intervention of French armies. His contempt for the masses was summed up by his rejection of a proposal from one of his lieutenants that the right to vote should be conceded in an occupied territory: 'It is ridiculous that you should quote against me the opinions of the people of Westphalia. If you listen to popular opinion, you will achieve nothing. If the people refuses its own happiness, the people is guilty of anarchy and deserves to be punished'. Despite the differences in the social systems upon which they rested, there are many similarities between the attitude of Stalin and the occupation of the Red Army in Eastern Europe in the post war period, and that of Napoleon 140 years previously. Both had issued from revolutions, and were covered in the authority of 'revolutionaries'. Stalin was a grey mediocrity, Napoleon a brilliant improviser. Nevertheless, there were certain common features in their regimes. When they occupied other countries, the model they turned to was not the heroic period of the revolution with the self-conscious organisation of the masses, but the bureaucratically controlled state in the case of Stalin, or the dictatorial regime in Napoleon's case. The bourgeoisie however had ceded power to Napoleon at a heavy price. On the one hand, as Marx and Engels pointed out:

> He fed the egoism of the French nation to complete satiety, but demanded also the sacrifice of bourgeois business, enjoyments, wealth, etc whenever this was required by the political aim of conquest. If he despotically suppressed the liberalism of bourgeois society—the political idealism of its daily practice—he showed no more consideration for its essential material interest, trade and industry, whenever they conflicted with his political interests. His scorn of industrial *hommes d'affaires* was the compliment to his scorn of ideologists. In his home policy, too, he combated bourgeois society as the opponent of the state which in his own person he still held to be an absolute aim in itself. Thus he declared in the State Council that he would not suffer the owner of extensive estates to cultivate them or not as he pleased. Thus, too, he conceived the plan of subordinating trade to the state by appropriation of *roulage* (road haulage). French businessmen took steps to anticipate the event that first shook Napoleon's power. Paris exchange brokers forced him by means of an artificially created famine to delay the opening of the Russian campaign by nearly two months and thus to launch it too late in the year.

Thus, while the regime of Napoleon rested on the bourgeoisie, he was not averse to striking blows at this class. The social base of Napoleon and the backbone of his army were the peasants. This army swept through Europe and, as is well known, right up to Moscow itself. The tale of Napoleon's military campaigns, its successes and his eventual defeat has been detailed many times. It is true that the retreat of the French armies from Russia back to *la patrie* in 1815 left in its wake a situation whereby the semi-feudal regimes remained intact. And yet the French conquering armies had shaken the old social order to its foundations and in turn laid a solid basis for the modern bourgeois state.

Thrown back on to the resources of France in 1814, he contemplated a revolutionary appeal to the people, the arming of the masses and the revival of the old cry of the 'Fatherland in danger'. However, after twelve years of virtually uninterrupted war, with the masses cowed and dispirited, they offered no resistance to the advancement of allied troops until the peasants were goaded into retaliation by the rapacious activities of the Cossacks and the Prussians who were advancing on Paris. Bordeaux surrendered without a fight to the English, and royalist agents were active everywhere. Finally, deserted by the Senate and Legislature and even by his own marshals who refused to serve him any longer, he was deposed. Louis XVIII, who promised a liberal charter, was invited to fill the throne. Bonaparte was exiled to Elba, but managed to keep in touch with events in France.

The king was installed on his throne with a marked lack of enthusiasm from the French people. The bourgeoisie, which had initially welcomed the return of Louis XVIII, were alarmed by the rumours which abounded that the monarch was about to restore sequestrated church and aristocratic property to their former owners. The army was also in a state of disaffection, with the dismissal on half pay of many of its officers. This created the conditions which allowed Napoleon to return to France on 20 March 1815. The king fled, and thus began Napoleon's famous 'one hundred days'.

Faced with a choice between appealing to the revolutionary traditions of the French nation and invoking the heroic period of 1793-94, or basing himself upon the bourgeoisie, he chose the latter. This did nothing to rally the republican and Jacobin tradition, still strong in France, to his side. However, 700,000 men were quickly mobilised and 120,000 took the field against the combined English and Prussian force led by Blucher and Wellington. Initially, he was successful in defeating Blucher's Prussians, but, confronted by Wellington at Waterloo, he was defeated. This in turn led to his second abdication, with the return of the king on 8 July in the baggage train of the Prussian army.

This time, savage reparations were inflicted on the French by the allies. Napoleon was subsequently exiled to St Helena, 5000 miles away from France where he died in 1821.

Obscuring the French revolution

Thus the French revolution, from its heroic beginnings and the overthrow of the monarchy and the institution of a democratic republic, had ended in the establishment of a military dictatorship, its subsequent defeat, the restoration of the monarchy and prostration at the feet of its European enemies.

Sages, bourgeois historians and their reformist shadows, will point to this as they do with all revolutions, as a means of discrediting the very concept of revolution itself as the locomotive of history. When confronted with a revolution, the dispossessed ruling class uses force—bullets, cannons and bayonets—in order to suppress and defeat it. Yet, once the revolution triumphs, the offensive against it assumes a different but not always a more subtle form! 'Intellectual' assaults on the revolution temporarily take the place of force or arms. Whole 'industries' spring up, armies of professors, whose sole purpose is to throw dust in the eyes of future generations as to the real meaning, impact and relevance of the revolution.

This applies not only to the French revolution but also to the British revolution of 1648. They point to the great French revolution as an example of the 'failure' of revolution in general as a method of taking society forward. It is true that, up to now, revolutions have never preserved all the gains won at the time of their highest peak. Following the making of the revolution by certain classes, groups, or individuals, others appear to profit from it. It appears that the reaction triumphs all along the line, in the case of France leading as we know to the restoration of the Bourbons. And yet, the revolution never goes back to its starting point. Thus, despite the return to the monarchy, the *ancien regime* had been shattered beyond the point of no return.

While the king created new titles and found new estates to reward returning emigrés, the land confiscated from the church and emigré nobles remained largely untouched. The new aristocracy under the Bourbon monarchy fused with the bourgeoisie in a new financial aristocracy. The gains of the bourgeois revolution remained intact.

The processes of the French revolution

The property relations established by the revolution allowed for the unfettered development of the bourgeoisie, which in turn created the proletariat which was to shake France to its foundations in the nineteenth century. Thus the French revolution passed through many phases and through many sharp turns.

The revolution of 1789 was the work primarily of the people of Paris and the other towns of France, backed up by a peasant war in the countryside. However, the revolution was not carried through to a conclusion and a period of dual power existed, between a weakened monarchy on the one side, and the revolutionary power on the other. This interregnum is maintained until 1791, coming to an end with the attempted flight of the king to Varennes in June of that year. This is followed by the massacre in the Champs de Mars in July 1791. The revolution is driven forward by the whip of the counter-revolution. The mass movement in turn raises the Gironde to power in early 1792. The Parisian masses invade the Tuileries amd force the king to wear the red bonnet and to drink the health of the nation. They are protesting against the use of his veto to check revolutionary legislation. This is a dress rehearsal for the insurrection later in the year.

Meanwhile, European counter-revolution declares war to the death, through the Brunswick manifesto, against the French revolution.

In August, 47 of the 48 sections in Paris demand the overthrow of the monarchy and the establishment of a republic. The sans-culottes, in conjunction with the petit bourgeois democrats in the Jacobins, organise the 10 August 'second French revolution'. The Assembly in turn votes to establish a National Convention and to draw up a new constitution.

Later in the month, allied troops enter France and Lafayette deserts to the enemy. They are halted in September at Valmy as the Legislative Assembly holds its last session and is replaced by the National Convention. On 21 September, the Convention votes unanimously to abolish the monarchy. Thus begins Year 1 of the republic.

In January 1793, the king is executed, but the Gironde, representing the big bourgeoisie, had compromised themselves by seeking an accommodation with the monarchy. They attack the Paris Commune, dominated as it is by the sans-culottes-Jacobin alliance. This in turn leads to the demonstrations of 31 May and June 2 which topple the Gironde from power.

The mass movement has raised on its back the Jacobin dictatorship, which lasts from June 1793 to 27 July (9 Thermidor) 1794. The revolution reaches its highest peak in Year 2 of the revolution.

The first period of Year 2 is characterised by a cementing of the alliance between the sans-culottes and the Jacobins, with the most democratic republican constitution yet seen. At the same time, the sans-culottes exercise the power in the Parisian sections, and collaborate with the Jacobins in the organisation of the revolutionary power throughout the country.

Due to their pressure, the Jacobin dictatorship accepts the famous *maximum général*, regulating food and other prices. However, the alliance betwen the sans-culottes and the Jacobins breaks down with the execution of the Hébertists and the weakening of the maximum, leading to widespread disillusionment and apathy. This is a factor which leads to the overthrow of Robespierre.

Far more critical, however, is the victory of French forces in occupied Belgium in the latter part of 1793. This is followed by other victories against the Spanish armies. Soon after the invasion of Italy and Savoy begins. With *la patrie* secured, the bourgeoisie turns against the emergency measures of the terror and its main proponent, Robespierre. With his execution the revolution goes into a descending curve.

The downswing is characterised, as with the upward curve, by outbreaks of civil war as the masses heroically attempt to cling to the gains which have accrued to them during the revolution. This is what the Germinal and Prairial uprisings in April and May 1795 respectively represent. Thermidor is a step along the road to the veiled dictatorship of the Directory, which in turn lays the basis for the establishment of the military-police dictatorship of Napoleon Bonaparte.

Bonapartism represents the triumph of bourgeois counter-revolution, but on the basis of the gains of the revolution itself. The Bonapartist regime is liquidated in 1815 by the entry of British and German troops into Paris and the restoration of the Bourbon monarchy.

Towards the socialist revolution!

In the manner in which bourgeois historians approach the French revolution, it represents merely an inexplicable jumble of events without any pattern or rhythm. Above all, the processes of the revolution are obscured. The reformists merely echo the bourgeois historians. Thus, a recent book, *Citizens* by Simon Schama, who claims to stand on the 'European left', writes:

> I am very bleak about 1789. As I encountered 1789 and 1790, I got more alarmed. For example, no sooner was the ink dry on the Declaration of the Rights of Man [in 1789] than the National Assembly -not the revolutionary Convention, remember, set up committees to report on potential counter-revolutionary plots and to open mail, stop people without warrant, detain people without due process and prevent freedom of movement.

He mournfully laments the execution of the governor of the Bastille:

> How do you explain the Governor of the Bastille's head being sawn through with a pen-knife and stuck on a pike?

Passed over are the hundreds who were shot down by the troops of this very governor. Incredibly, this method is, it seems, 'a liberating thing. You are so much more empowered to attack Mrs Thatcher or to say "Of course there is an alternative to the

Right" if you are honest with your own history.' Thus 'honesty with your own history' is equal in Schama's book with agreeing with the bourgeois calumniators of the French masses. Completely ignored is the ferocious and bloody counter-revolutionary attacks on the revolution which were *entirely* the cause of any counter-violence by the masses themselves. Only Marxism is capable of tracing the thread of the French revolution, the processes which evolve at each stage, and the interconnection between the great personalities of the revolution and how they affect and are in turn affected by the revolutionary process itself.

Schama is not at all original in lamenting the 'excesses' of the masses, while passing over in silence the crimes of counter-revolution. Plekhanov, who wrote a brilliant critique of the French revolution, nevertheless lectured the Russian masses in 1905 and bemoaned their resorting to 'arms'. This attempt of Schama, only the latest in a long litany of attacks on the revolutionary masses in the French revolution, cannot obscure their great progressive historical mission.

When their descendants, the mighty French proletariat, moved in their millions in 1830, in 1834-35, in 1848 and in 1871, and in the earth-shattering revolutionary events in France in the twentieth century, it would be to the giants of the French revolution to whom they would turn for inspiration.

It is only through the mighty labours of the Parisian sans-culottes that the ground was cleared for the development of industry and society, of the working class and of the mighty modern labour movement. Therefore, in every sense, the working class movement today stands on their sturdy shoulders. They yearned and struggled mightily for a society where want and privation would be abolished. The material means were not at hand 200 years ago. Now, the colossal development of the productive forces makes it possible for the first time in history to abolish poverty, despoliation of the environment and misery from the whole of the planet. In forging the weapons to create such a world, the working class today, not just in France, but throughout the world, could enormously benefit by studying the great French revolution and the role of the masses in that mighty event.

Appendix on democracy in the French Revolution

THE FRENCH revolution established the most advanced democratic republic that the world up to then had seen. This was achieved through an alliance of the revolutionary bourgeoisie with the plebeian sans-culottes. However, the latter, as we have seen, were prepared to go much further than the bourgeoisie in the field of democracy. In some respects, the sans-culottes anticipated the demands which the workers in the Paris Commune were to formulate in 1871 and upon which Karl Marx based his ideas for a democratic workers' state.

According to the Parisian section la Cité, popular sovereignty was 'imprescriptible, inalienable, and indelegable'. Albert Soboul comments in his valuable book *Understanding the French Revolution*: 'From that the sans-culottes drew a conclusion that constituted one of the levers of popular action: censure, control and recall of elected officials'. The timid leaders of the Labour movement today are put in the shade by the sans-culottes when it comes to democracy. The sans-culottes drew inspiration from Rousseau who had criticised the British parliamentary and electoral system: 'If the English people think they are free, they deceive themselves; they are only free during the election of members of Parliament; as soon as these are elected, the people are slaves; they no longer count for anything...The deputies of the people thus are not nor can they be the people's representatives; they are only their commissioners'.

The sans-culottes were even opposed to calling the deputies in the Convention 'representatives'. Instead they used the term 'proxies', that is they held power on behalf, by 'proxy', of the people. Thus, the Tuileries Section in 1792 declared that: 'The deputies must not be called representatives, but proxies of the people'. Leclerc in *L'Ami du Peuple* in 1793 declared: 'A represented people is not free...Don't lavish this epithet of representatives...The will of the people cannot be represented'. When the sans-culottes wrote to their deputies in Year Two of the Revolution, they invariably signed their messages, 'Your equal under the law'. Some denounced the system of two-tiered elections, with the most advanced Sections demanding direct universal suffrage. Lacroix, in a paper to the Marseilles section, denounced the two-tiered voting as 'immoral, destructive to the sovereignty of the people, favourable to intrigues and cabals'. The Quinze-Vingts Section, which was one of the most radical, at one stage approved a plan which stated that: 'there be no electoral bodies, but that any elections be held in the primary assemblies'.

However, the sans-culottes were not satisfied with opposition to two-tiered elections or upholding the principle of popular sovereignty. They were insistent in demanding the implementation of the principle of control and recall of elected officials by the 'sovereign people'. Thus, in 1792 the Marche-des-Innocents section demanded that in elections to the

National Convention: 'The deputies will be subject to recall at the will of their departments', and that 'Public officials will be subject to recall by those who appointed them, whose deliberations they will be obliged to execute'. Many others such as the Les Halles Section supported them, while the Droits-de-l'Homme declared that it was reserving the right to recall deputies 'If in the course of the session, they demonstrated signs of lack of patriotism'. In the battle between the Girondins and the Montagnards from the Autumn of 1792 onwards, the advanced Sections demanded the right to censure elected officials and to demand an accounting from them, while according to Soboul, 'The moderate sections protested against this claim'.

On 10 March 1793, in the struggle against the Girondins in the Convention, the Cordeliers Club demanded the exercise of 'popular sovereignty' to replace 'the members who are traitors to the cause of the people'. The Quatre-Nations Section interpreted this as a call to 'recall the unfaithful proxies, unworthy of being legislators of the public welfare, since they have betrayed their mandate by voting for the preservation of the tyrant and the appeal to the people'. At the same time the sans-culottes completely rejected the bourgeois concept of the 'inviolability' of parliamentarians. This they considered 'as being an odious privilege to betray the interests of the people with impunity, a perfidious cloak with which a corrupt proxy can cover himself'. Not much respect here for 'Parliamentary privileges'!

Even the Jacobins, the most revolutionary wing of the bourgeoisie, violently denounced and suppressed the 'direct democracy' of the sans-culottes once they had taken power. The sans-culottes were way ahead of the present leaders of the Labour movement in voting, also. Thus, according to Soboul:

> It was the practice of voting by voice or by acclamation. The sans-culottes felt that the patriot had nothing to hide, neither his opinions nor his actions. Political life thus unfolded in broad daylight, under the eyes of the people; the administrative bodies and the section assemblies deliberated in public sessions, the electors voted by voice vote with the tribunes watching: one acted in secret only if one had evil designs. 'Publicity is the safeguard of the people'.

In the Kinnock dominated British Labour Party the practice of 'secretive ballots' has become the norm. Of course the 'secret ballot' for parliamentary and other elections has historically evolved as a means of avoiding coercion of the voters by the ruling powers, dictatorial governments etc. However, such safeguards against 'undue pressure' should not be necessary within the labour movement today. These practices are invariably resorted to by the conservative officialdom which dominates the labour movement in order to preserve their position and cushion themselves against mass criticisms. On the National Executive Committee for instance the previous practice of automatic recorded votes has been watered down. This is not a step in the direction of greater democracy but is done in order to screen the right-wing NEC representatives from the rank and file who elected them. The same practices are commonplace in the Trade Unions. Real democracy would mean voting openly with full accountability to the ordinary members.

Contrast this to the democracy of the sans-culottes. In 1792, one of the Sections in its Assembly elected a new president and declared the voice vote 'the only ballot appropriate to republicans'. With the voice vote went the ballot by acclamation, with sitting or rising becoming the norm in the Assemblies. As Soboul comments: 'It soon seemed the only method of revolutionary balloting'.

Thus, in the Parisian sections, the revolutionary committees were elected in March 1793 by the voice vote, accompanied by sitting or rising. During the election in May 1793 for the Chief of the Parisian National Guard, which resulted in the election of Hanriot, the method was by voice vote in the Sections. The moderates (shades of the right wing in the labour movement today) denounced this method and were for the secret ballot! The moderates had the 'law' on their side which did not support the idea of the voice vote. The sans-culottes, however, had a greater 'law', in the form of a mass movement. Through the method of voice vote the power and influence of the sans-culottes grew enormously. It was not just because of urgency that the sans-culottes adopted these methods: 'It was, apart from a means of annihilating opponents, a manifestation of revolutionary unity dear to the sans-culottes.' This practice was the rule until the spring of Year Two. In the General Assembly of the Butte-des-Moulins in November 1793, it was decided 'to proceed to nominations in a revolutionary manner by sitting and rising; on 15 December it re-elected its officers in a revolutionary manner by acclamation'. At the same time:

> Voting by acclamation was finally imposed, under popular pressure, on the General Council of the Commune. On 20 February 1794, Lubin, its president, asked to be replaced. 'Lubin! Lubin!' shouted the members of the Council, almost unanimously, and the gallery took up the cry: 'Lubin! Lubin!' Lubin observed that such a nomination would not be legal. The laws of the provisional government were consulted; it was determined that the General Council had the right to name and to re-elect its president when it pleased and in the manner in which it pleased. 'Nominate canvassers, proceed to the ballot? That would take up too much time'. Lubin was proclaimed elected.

However, with the move to the right of the Jacobins and with the suppression of the Cordeliers in February-March 1794, voting by acclamation and voice vote was outlawed. Thus, even in the bourgeois French revolution, the democratic aspirations of the plebeian masses clashed with even the most revolutionary wing of the bourgeois. The sans-culottes were suppressed, but their demands were once more to arise in the 19th century with the emergence of the French proletariat.

Bibliography

Below is a list of the main sources used in the production of this book, including those from which the main quotations have been taken.

E Belfort Bax: *The last episode French Revolution*
Edmund Burke: *Reflections on the revolution in France*
Thomas Carlyle: *The French Revolution*
John L Carr: *Robespierre: the force of circumstance*
C Cipollo (ed):   *Fontana Economic History of Europe*
A Cobban: *Social Interpretation of the French Revolution*
A Cobban: *Aspects of the French Revolution*
Vincent Cronin: *Louis and Antoinette*
William Doyle: *Origins of the French Revolution*
Frederick Engels: *Socialism, Utopian and Scientific*
Frederick Engels: *Kautsky on the French Revolution*
Bernard Fay: *Louis XVI or The End of a World*
CH George: *Revolution: 5 Centuries of Europe in Conflict*
Jacques Godechot: *Taking of the Bastille: July 14 1789*
Pierre Goubert: *The ancien regime*
N Hampson: *Social History of the French Revolution*
Felice Harcourt: *Memoirs of Madame de la Tour du Pin*
John Hearsay: *Marie Antoinette*
E J Hobsbawm: *The Age of Revolution*
Ralph Korngold: *Robespierre: First Modern Dictator*
PA Kropotkin: *The Great French Revolution*
Georges Lefebvre: *The coming of the French Revolution*
Georges Lefebvre: *The French Revolution 2 Vols*
VI Lenin: Articles in *Pravda* 7.7.1917
R Levasseur: *Memoirs*
Karl Marx: Articles in the *Neue Rheinische Zeitung*
Marx and Engels: *Collected Works Vol 3; The Holy Family*
Thomas Paine: *The Rights of Man*
G Plekhanov: *The Bourgeois Revolution*
G Plekhanov: *Development of the Monist View of History*
G Plekhanov: *The Role of the Individual in History*
JJ Rousseau: *The Social Contract and Discourses*
George Rudé: *The Crowd in the French Revolution*
George Rudé: *The face of the Crowd; Revolutionary Europe*
George Rudé: *Europe in the Eighteenth Century*
John Scott (trans):   *The defense of Gracchus Babeuf*
Albert Soboul: *Understanding the French Revolution*
Charles Tilley: *The Vendee*
Alexis de Tocqueville: *The ancien regime*
Claire Tomalin: *Life and Death of Mary Wollstonecraft*
Leon Trotsky: *History of the Russian Revolution*
Leon Trotsky: *1905; On Britain*
Leon Trotsky: *Writings 1935-36, 1936-37, 1938*
Leon Trotsky: *Terrorism and Communism*
Leon Trotsky: *Challenge of the Left Opposition 3 Vols*

Glossary of French terms

Ami du peuple, L': founded by Marat in September 1789 circulated widely among the people. Often suppressed, it changed its name to *Publiciste de la République francaise* in March 1793. The last issue appeared the day after Marat's murder.

armee révolutionnaire: armed force of Jacobins and *sans-culottes* raised in the late summer of 1793. Its principal purpose was to force farmers to release their stocks for Paris and other towns. It was disbanded after the executions of the Hébertists.

assignats: interest-bearing bonds which—with a face value of 1,000 *livres* each—were intended to be used in payment for former church land. *Assignats* stopped bearing interest in May 1791; and, by the time of the Directory, 100 *livres* in *assignats* were worth no more than fifteen *sous*.

barrieres: customs posts surrounding Paris.

Brissotins: the name by which the Girondins were at first more usually known, after Brissot.

cahiers de doléances: lists of grievances drawn up by each of the three orders before the meeting of the Estates General in 1789.

'Ca ira!': revolutionary song. First heard in Paris during the preparations for the *Fête de la Fédération* of 14 July 1790. The refrain, which was said to have been written by a street-singer named Ladre, originally ran:

> *Ah! Ca ira, ca ira, ca ira!*
> *Le peuple, en ce jour, sans cesse repete:*
>
> *(Here we go, here we go, here we go*
> *The people, on this day, with this chorus).*

The words were altered during the Terror to:

> *Ah! Ca ira, ca ira, ca ira!*
> *Les aristocrates a la lanterne!*

capitation: poll-tax levied in rough correspondence to income. Established in 1701. The clergy bought themselves out in 1710 for 24 million *livres*. The nobility had also become exempt by the time of the Revolution and the *capitation* was levied only on commoners.

Champs de Mars: originally the chief military parade ground of Paris.

Chouans: royalist insurgents who took their name from four brothers named Cottereau, known more often as Chouan. *Chouans* were active in La Vendée, Brittany and Normandy.

comités de surveillance: watch-committees formed in each commune in March 1793 to keep an eye on officialdom and supervise public security and order. They were usually controlled by extreme Jacobins and often took the place of local government. They later became known as *comités révolutionnaires* and after *Thermidor* as *comités d'arrondissements*.

145

Commune: the revolutionary local government authority of Paris. It was formed in July 1789 and disbanded after *Thermidor*. The official Commune on 9 August 1792, the day before the attack on the Tuileries.

Cordeliers: A Parisian district inhabited by many actors, playwrights, booksellers, publishers, printers and journalists, Marat and Camille Desmoulins among them. Danton also lived here.

Cordeliers' Club (Society of the Friends of the Rights of Man and of the Citizen): formed when the Commune redivided Paris and the Cordeliers' District was absorbed into the *section* Théâtre-Francais. The Cordeliers' Club was generally more radical than the Jacobins, after 10 August 1792 the more moderate members such as Danton and Desmoulins stopped attending, and the *Enragés* began to dominate it.

corvées royales: direct taxes paid in service rather than money.

Enragés: extreme revolutionaries, led by Jacques Roux and Jean Varlet, who became a powerful force in Paris in 1793. They were particularly antagonistic to those suspected of hoarding or speculating.

faubourgs: former suburbs originally outside the walls of Paris but by the time of the revolution they had all been enclosed within the city's boundaries.

fédéres: the citizen soldiers who came to Paris from the provinces for the Festival of the Federation on 14 July 1792. Prominent among them were units from Brest and the men from Marseilles who popularized the *Marseillaise*.

Fermiers généraux: paid large sums for the right to collect various indirect taxes and made fortunes by exploiting them.

Feuillants: constitutional monarchists who resigned from the Jacobin Club in July 1791 in protest against moves to have the King deposed.

gabelle: the government salt monopoly by which people were made to buy specific amounts of salt at prices far higher than they would have fetched on an open market.

Garde Nationale: the citizens' militia which was formed by the Paris districts in 1789. Originally a predominantly bourgeois institution. Its character changed as the revolution progressed.

Gardes-francaises: royal troops stationed in the capital when the revolution began. Most of them proved sympathetic towards the masses in the July 1789 insurrection.

Girondins: Name originally given to a group of deputies in the Assembly who supported Brissot's policy of a 'revolutionary war' in 1791. Many came from the Gironde region. Later the name applied to a wider group in opposition to the main body of Jacobins.

Indulgents: those, who advocated a policy of clemency during the height of the First Terror.

Jacobin Club: founded at Versailles in 1789 and then known as the Breton Club as most of its members came from Brittany. On the removal of the

Assembly to Paris it became known as the Jacobin Club because it met in the convent of the Jacobin friars. In 1791 the Club was named *Société des amis de la constitution, séante aux Jacobins* and after the fall of the monarchy *Société des Jacobins amis de la liberté et de l'égalité*. The Club became increasingly revolutionary. It was closed in November 1795.

jeunesse dorée: gangs of young anti-Jacobins, armed with whips and weighted sticks, who were encouraged by Fréron to attack left-wing agitators and recalcitrant workers.

journée: an important day, particularly one upon which some action of revolutionary significance occurred.

lanterne: a lamppost which served as a gibbet in the early part of the Revolution.

levée en masse: the mobilization of the country's total human and material resources. It was approved reluctantly by the Convention on 23 August 1793.

livre: unit of weight and monetary value. 20 *sous* = 1 *livre*. According to the journalist Linguet (1736-94) a man needed 300 *livres* a year to live in reasonable comfort.

maximum: declaration of maximum prices. The *maximum* of May 1793 imposed a limit on the price of grain only, that of September 1793 on most essential articles. The *maximum* was abolished in December 1794. Many shopkeepers had flagrantly disregarded it.

Montagnards: Jacobin deputies, collectively known as the Mountain, who occupied the higher seats in the Convention. Originally led by Danton and Robespierre, they helped to form the government after the overthrow of the Girondins.

Pere Duchesne: Hébert's irreverent journal which appeared three times a week between 1790 and 1794.

Plain: the group in the Convention, also known as the Marsh or *Marais*, that occupied the middle ground between Girondins and Jacobins.

sans-culottes: literally 'without breeches', breeches were a form of dress associated with aristocrats and the well-to-do; workers wore trousers. The term had political as well as economic significance. Numerous shopkeepers and master craftsmen who read revolutionary newspapers and pamphlets and influenced their illiterate workmen liked to be considered *sans-culottes*. But *sans-culottes* were generally poor.

sections: before the Revolution, Paris was divided into sixty districts. The Commune redivided it into forty-eight *sections*. Each had its own revolutionary committee and armed force upon which it could rely in times of trouble.

taille: basic tax of the French monarchy during the *ancien régime* which varied from province to province. The privileged and influential managed to escape paying it so that in practice it was paid almost entirely by the poor, principally the peasants.

vingtieme: originally intended as a five per cent tax on income, by the time of the revolution it was mostly paid by the peasants.

Index

INDEX

Booklist

World Socialist Books is a book service for the Labour movement. Listed below are some of the books on the French revolution currently in print. In addition to these, we can supply many other books on history, politics, Trade Union matters, and the struggle for socialism in general.

E J Hobsbawm	*The Age of Revolution*..	£5.99
Charles Dickens	*A Tale of Two Cities.*	£1.25
Claire Tomalin	*Life & Death of Wollstonecraft.*	£5.99
P Kropotkin	*Great French Revolution (2 vols).*	£3.95 each
Thomas Carlyle	*The French Revolution.*	£7.95
George Rudé	*Revolutionary Europe..*	£4.95
George Rudé	*Europe in the 18th Century..*	£8.95
George Rudé	*The Crowd in History.*	£5.95
George Rudé	*Crowd in the French Revolution.*	£5.95
Thomas Paine	*The Rights of Man.*	£3.50
CLR James	*The Black Jacobins.*	£5.99
Albert Soboul	*Understanding the French Revolution*	£7.95
Leon Trotsky	*History of the Russian Revolution.*	£8.00
Leon Trotsky	*Terrorism and Communism.*	£4.95
F Engels	*Socialism: Utopian and Scientific.*	£0.60

All of the above books can be obtained by writing to:
World Socialist Books, 3/13 Hepscott Road, London E9 5HB.

Special Offers from FORTRESS BOOKS

The Unbroken Thread
The Development of Trotskyism over 40 years—Selected writings of Ted Grant

608 pages, many photos
Special offer, the Hardback (cover price £11.95) for the softback price £6.95. 5 copies for £30
An invaluable collection of Marxist writings covering 1938-83, charting the development of Marxist ideas through the 1939-45 war, the rise of Stalinism in Eastern Europe, the post war boom, the colonial revolution and the crisis of British capitalism.

Month of Revolution
by Clare Doyle

80 pages, £1.95 (cover price £2.50). 5 copies for £8
A vivid account of the tumultuous events in France 1968.

Liverpool—A City That Dared to Fight
by Peter Taaffe and Tony Mulhearn

528 pages. Hardback £9.95 (cover price £14.95)
Softback £6.95, 5 copies for £25
'A fascinating self-portrait...told with imagery redolent of Petrograd 1917.' *The Independent 25/1/88*

Out of the Night
by Jan Valtin

712 pages, hardback only £7.95 (cover price £9.95), 5 copies for £35
A classic socialist autobiography, outlining the life and struggles of a Communist Party trade union activist in Germany 1918-38.

Germany—From Revolution to Counter Revolution
by Rob Sewell

96 pages, £2 (cover price £2.50). 5 copies for £8.50
Covers events in Germany from the 1918 revolution to the rise of Hitler in 1933, drawing out the lessons for the movement today.

Order from World Socialist Books, or direct from Fortress Books, PO Box 141 London E2 ORL. Postage—please add 20% on orders under £5, 10% on orders £5-£10. Over £10 post free.